Published by Whisker & Wing Publishing

Walnut Creek, California

www.whiskerandwing.com

This is a work of nonfiction. Names and identifying details may have been changed to protect the privacy of individuals.

Printed in the United States of America

First Edition

ISBN: 979-8-9998479-0-4

Library of Congress Control Number: 20259118663

Contents

To the ones still circling the question.

To the ones who've answered it out loud.

And to the ones who sat beside us while we figured it out.

Prologue

Not all women want kids.

Some never did.
Some thought they did.
Some still don't know.

This book is for all of them. To say:

You're not alone.
You're not wrong.
You're not less of a woman.
And you get to decide what your life looks like.

This book isn't a memoir. It's a gathering place. A chorus. A soft-landing place for women from all walks of life who found themselves childfree.

This isn't a story of waking up one day and knowing. It's a story of sitting with the grief of not knowing, and later, with the quiet truth that I would never be the mom I once thought I'd be. And somehow, still finding peace.

If the tone shifts from chapter to chapter, it's because this journey isn't linear. It certainly wasn't for me.

Even while writing this book, I found myself grieving again at times, and at other times, completely rejoicing. There's no single path to arrive at this decision. It looks different for everyone.

You'll find pieces of my story, yes. But also:

•Stories from real women from all over the world.

•Research and data to show you this is more common than you think.

•Humor, because we need it.

•Honesty, because we deserve it.

•And above all, compassion.

For the version of you that wanted to want kids.
For the version of you that always knew you didn't.
For the version of you still figuring it out.

Some chapters may not apply to you. That's okay. This book isn't here to speak for you. It's here to sit with you.

Why I Wrote This

I spent most of my life on the fence.

When I finally started coming to terms with my decision that I didn't want children, I went looking for a book that could make me feel seen. Less alone. Valued. Supported.

I found pieces. Stories that came close. But I never quite heard myself in them.

So, I set out to write the book I needed in those moments. The unsure ones, the certain ones, the ones where I felt judged, embarrassed, ashamed, or quietly relieved.

I went looking for other voices from all walks of life who could help me build this book. Some never wanted kids. Some thought they did. Some still don't know. But they were all brave enough to share their stories, and I'm so grateful they did. For privacy, you'll meet them here under different names. My hope is that somewhere in these pages, one of these voices finds you right when you need it most.

To the Reader Who's on the Fence

This book isn't here to persuade you one way or another. It's here to empower you. To say loudly and proudly, that your decision is no one's choice, and no one's business, but your own.

To the Reader Who Has Fully Embraced a Childfree Life

This book is a celebration of you and your choice. Of the freedom, fulfillment, and self-trust it takes to build a life that's truly yours.

To the Reader Who is a Friend, Partner, or Relative of Someone Who is Childfree

This book is an invitation to see their choice through a new lens. To hear the thoughts they may have struggled to voice. To understand that this is deeply personal, and to thank you for being open enough to try.

To the Reader Who Wanted Children and Couldn't Have Them

I want to honor you directly. This book centers on the experience of being childfree by choice. I can't speak to the grief of infertility, and I won't pretend to. But some of the voices you'll meet in these pages do come from women whose paths to childfree began with loss, treatment fatigue, timing, health, or circumstances beyond their control. If parts of this book sting, please skip freely. If parts resonate, take them with you. I'm glad you're here.

A Quick Reality Check

According to a recent report by Morgan Stanley, nearly 45% of U.S. women aged 25 to 44 will be single and childfree by 2030. It's one of the most significant cultural shifts in modern history, driven by rising costs of living, expanding career ambitions, delayed partnerships, and a re-evaluation of what fulfillment means.

It's not about hating marriage or rejecting motherhood. It's about asking: What if there's more than one version of a good life?

Globally, the shift is happening, too. A 39-country global study found that 18% of adult women said they don't have children and don't plan to.

But we still don't talk about it.

Not openly. Not honestly.

And certainly not without judgment.

You are not weird. You are not rare.

You are part of a growing community that deserves to be seen, respected, and celebrated.

Welcome

If you've ever questioned whether you're selfish, off-track, bitter, or confused for not wanting children, let me be the one to say it: You're not. You're brave.

And you're about to hear from a whole community of women who feel the same.

Section One: The In-Between

Some decisions are easy.

This isn't one of them.

This isn't the clarity section. It's the section before that. The tug-of-war between "*maybe*," "*probably not*", and "*wait, should I want this?*".

It's about the quiet guilt of not feeling guilty. The fear that you're missing some maternal gene everyone else seems to have. The pressure to explain yourself before you even fully understand your own answer.

You might see yourself in one chapter and not in another. That's the point.

This isn't a well-lit path. It's a maze. And there's no right way through it, only your way.

These are the messy, tender, deeply personal moments where many of us start.

And you don't need to have it all figured out to start feeling at peace.

Chapter 1

The Mother of All Questions

"Do I even want kids?"

There was a time in my life when I couldn't tell if I wanted to be a mom, or if I just didn't want to be the only one who wasn't.

Afraid that my secret judgment of myself, that internal scream of *"you're selfish"*, would suddenly come to light and that's all anyone would see in me.

Everyone else was doing it. Friends were getting pregnant on purpose.

Even the girl from high school who I once saw snort cocaine in the bathroom during lunch was now somebody's mother.

Meanwhile, I was sitting in my living room surrounded by cat toys, wondering if it's wrong to love the life I already have.

The question *"Do I want kids?"* didn't show up as a whisper.

It was loud. Obsessive. Hormonal.

A late-20s, early-30s identity crisis that had me Googling things like:

"How to know if you want to be a mom."

"Will my parents resent me if I don't give them grandkids?"

"Is 'not hating kids' the same as wanting one?"

Some days I thought maybe I did want a baby.

Like when I saw a group of moms sitting outside a coffee shop with their strollers parked beside them.

They looked so...grounded.

Tired, sure. Messy buns, yoga pants, spit up on their shirts, but still tethered to something real.

They looked so adult.

I was their age, maybe even older, but in those moments seeing groups of women like this, I felt lightyears behind.

Not because I hadn't accomplished anything, but because their lives had gravity. And the only stroller I own is for my cats.

They had found their people. Their rhythm. Their identity wasn't floating in the ether anymore. It was anchored.

I was successful. Independent. Loved. But in those moments, I felt...untethered.

Like I was still blueprinting my life while they'd already broken ground.

I didn't necessarily want what they had.

I just wanted to stop questioning everything I didn't have.

And then there were the hockey games.

There's something about seeing a toddler in a tiny Sharks jersey that hits me right in the heart. The kind of hit that makes your uterus yell, "I NEED THAT!"

I'd see a dad hoist his kid on his shoulders, or a mom with face paint and matching jerseys for her and her little one, and something in me would ache. It reminded me of when my dad used to take my brother and me to Sharks games as kids.

Well, kind of take us.

In true 90s parenting fashion, he'd buy two tickets, hand them to us like little grown-ups, and send us into the arena alone. Then he'd sneak around to some side door and meet us at our seats like that was just how things worked.

The 90s were a great decade.

There's a warmth in those memories that made me wonder if I wanted to recreate them.

To have a mini-me who loved what I loved. Who inherited my weird superstitions about lucky jerseys and pre-game sandwiches.

Someone I could pass the torch to.

But even that wasn't really about raising a child. It was about legacy. Belonging. The romantic idea of seeing your quirks reflected back in someone else's face. It was nostalgia, dressed up as a future.

But those weren't true desires for motherhood.

They were cravings. For connection. For comfort. For identity.

For someone to love me unconditionally.

My desire to feel important. A desire to matter.

I realized that my interest in motherhood was always limited to the highlight reel. The cute clothes. The giggles. The photo-worthy moments. I never pictured the 5 a.m. wakeups, the years of constant supervision once they're mobile, the endless "why?" questions, the backtalk stage, or the ache when they inevitably pull away. I wanted the easy parts, and obviously I knew that wasn't the whole job description.

That's when I had to get honest with myself.

It made me feel exactly what I didn't want to feel. Selfish.

Like I was failing some kind of invisible womanhood test that everyone else had already passed with flying colors.

But here's the truth:

Recognizing that didn't make me selfish.

It made me self-aware.

Selfish would've been knowing all that and doing it anyway.

I knew I'd actually make a damn good mother.

I'm fiercely protective. Emotionally tuned in. A good mix of gentle and don't-test-me. I'm a perfectionist. I take care of what's mine.

I don't think parenthood would have broken me.

But it would've swallowed me whole.

Because motherhood is relentless.

There's no "done." No gold stars. No off-switch. No sick days.

And I knew myself well enough to know I would try to be perfect at it, which is a fast track to burnout. Or resentment.

Still, no one saw that inner calculation.

They just saw someone maternal-adjacent and made assumptions.

So, when family, friends, or boyfriends would say things like, "*You'll be such a good mom someday*", it didn't feel like the compliment they intended.

It felt like a task I must live up to. And that just put more pressure on me as I wondered if something was wrong with me for not wanting it as much as other people around me.

The question was never if I'd be good at it.

The question was if I wanted it.

And for years, I didn't know the answer.

I looked for signs.

I've taken pregnancy tests that I secretly hoped were positive. Probably not because I wanted a baby, but because I thought it would finally awaken the natural urge in me to want kids.

It would validate my life. Give me permission to stop doubting myself for doing it all wrong.

Other times, I hoped hard for a negative, because deep down, I knew I didn't want it.

Because my body hurt. My energy was limited.

I loved my sleep. My weekends. My peace.

I liked my life.

But was liking your life enough of a reason to say no to motherhood?

Would I regret it?

Would I wake up at 53 and wish I'd made a different choice?

Was I defective? Bitter? Confused?

Or still just "*not there yet*"?

Because we're taught to want this.

Taught that motherhood is the next step, the right step, the natural step.

And if you don't want it, you must be selfish. Or lacking. Or unnatural.

But it doesn't have to mean any of those things.

Choosing not to have kids can be an act of love, not avoidance.

For me, it was choosing to love the life I could actually give my best to.

A decision made from clarity, not confusion.

It can be bold. Brave.

Freeing.

And I eventually got there.

It didn't mean I hated kids.

It didn't mean I'd never feel a flicker of "*what if?*"

It just meant I stopped trying to contort myself into the life everyone else seemed to want and started listening to my inner doubts about taking that path.

And for the first time, my life started to feel like mine.

But even after I made peace with my decision, a new question crept in.

If this is really what I want, why do I feel sad?

Chapter 2
The Grief That Set Me Free

"I thought I was mourning a person. Turns out, I was mourning a path I never really wanted."

There's a moment I remember vividly, not because it was dramatic, but because it was quiet.

I was alone in my new apartment, a few months after a breakup that nearly unraveled me.

We'll call him Justin.

We'd been together for over six years. And for much of that time, we talked about marriage and kids. Not constantly, but enough that it became a running theme. Sometimes a hope, sometimes a negotiation, sometimes a full-blown fight.

It was part of our rhythm. Something we circled around without ever landing on.

Meanwhile, I felt time moving fast and my body moving slower.

I have rheumatoid arthritis, or RA, an autoimmune disease that's taught me my limits the hard way.

There are medications that may have helped me that I've turned down because of pregnancy risks. "Maybe baby" conversations with doctors that always ended in shrugs of my indecision.

Once, my rheumatologist casually mentioned that some women with RA go into remission during pregnancy and I practically sprinted home to Justin like, *"I'm ready to get pregnant immediately!"*

But I refrained.

Quiet timelines lived in my head. Not just related to my age, but about joint pain, energy crashes, and how long I could keep pushing through before my body just said no.

My biological clock wasn't a hum.

It was a goddamn ticking timebomb strapped to my uterus.

So, when that relationship ended when I was 33, it didn't feel like just a breakup.

It felt like everything I'd spent my adult life building had just collapsed.

I didn't just lose him. I lost the plan. The direction. The version of my life I had mapped out in Sharpie.

And here's the part that's hard to say out loud:

I was so fucking relieved.

Not at first. At first, I was wrecked. I grieved that breakup with everything in me.

I felt like I'd failed as a partner, as a woman.

But in the silence, after the crying stopped, and the therapy and anti-depressants kicked in, a deeper truth surfaced. The kind you only hear when all the noise dies down.

I realized I didn't actually want the life I'd been chasing.

I wanted certainty.
I wanted proof I was doing it right.
I wanted a clean, presentable answer when someone asked, *"So what's next for you?"*

But kids? That was never the dream.

That was just the expectation.

The checkbox I thought I was supposed to reach before 35 or risk becoming someone that people quietly pitied.

Chloe, a woman I interviewed while writing this book, said it perfectly.

"I did a little bit of grieving what the life I always thought I'd have wouldn't be anymore. It's just so ingrained in us, especially as women."

Exactly.

I wasn't grieving the absence of a baby.

I was grieving the idea that I'd never become someone I never actually wanted to be.

And that grief was real.

But so was the freedom that followed.

You can mourn something and be glad it's gone.

You can let go of a dream and still be grateful you never lived it.

Grief and relief can share the same page.

And for some women, there's no grief at all. Just clarity.

Another woman I spoke to, Amanda, told me this when I asked if she ever felt guilt about not having children:

"Over not having kids? Never. Only for the fact that I didn't feel guilt made me sometimes feel guilty. As if something was wrong with me for not wanting them."

That one hit me.

Because yes. That guilt.

The guilt for not feeling guilty.

The internal voice that whispers, *"Shouldn't you feel some sort of remorse about this?"*

I've heard versions of that over and over.

Women who never felt the tug. Never imagined nurseries. Never picked out baby names in their heads.

Women who looked around and thought, *"Am I the only one not hearing this clock?"*

And yet, they were still told they were selfish. Cold. Confused. *"Not there yet."*

As if there's only one destination, and if you're not rushing toward it, you must be lost.

What I've come to understand is this: all of it is valid.

The women who grieve.

The women who don't.

The ones who feel both, sometimes in the same breath.

The ones who never even had to ask the question.

If you've ever wondered why you don't feel more sad, or why you do, this chapter is for you.

Not because I have your answer, but because I've lived both.

It's okay if you grieve the version of you who once thought might be a mom.

It's okay if you don't.

It's okay if your grief shows up randomly on a Tuesday afternoon.

Or never arrives at all.

It's okay if you feel relief wrapped in sadness.

Or sadness wrapped in relief.

Or if you still can't tell them apart.

This isn't a test.

There's no right answer.

There's just your truth, however quiet, however complicated.

And there's no wrong way to feel your way through it.

Chapter 3

Cute, But Not For Me

"I'm not a dog person."

I feel the same way about kids as I do about dogs.

I like them in theory. From a distance. When they belong to someone else.

When I see a happy kid or a floppy-eared golden retriever, I think, aw, that's cute. But then I look at the person holding the leash or hovering near the scooter and that's when the feeling shifts. Because the kid (or the dog) usually looks thrilled. The adult looks...tired. Distracted. Slightly dead inside.

It's not a judgment. It's an observation.

I was reminded of this just the other day while doing the dishes. My neighbor across the street was standing in her front yard while her two young boys played in the street. It was a classic suburban scene. Kids on bikes and a mom watching from a distance. And yet, all I could think was how I do not envy her on this Friday evening.

She wasn't doing anything out of the ordinary. But the look on her face said it all. A mix of annoyance, fake enthusiasm, low-battery energy, and the mental checklist of all the things she probably wasn't going to have enough time or energy to do that night, weekend, or maybe even for the next 18 or so years.

I dried my hands, looked out the window again, and felt a wave of gratitude. I wasn't responsible for anything, unless you count two cats who nap all day, don't need walks, and never ask me to watch them ride a bicycle. I didn't have to plan dinner around anyone's bedtime but my own. I didn't have to pretend that standing on a lawn at sunset while mediating a squabble over helmet colors was my idea of a satisfying end to the week.

Instead, I just...did whatever the hell I wanted for the rest of the night. Because I could. And it's in those moments that the decision to be childfree feels so deeply right.

Of course, I know there are good moments that come with having kids. I'm not denying that. But when I picture myself in their shoes, well, the shoes feel tight. Like they were never my size.

For a long time, I told myself I'd feel different if it were my kid. Or my dog. That once the responsibility was mine, I'd understand the joy. I'd step into those shoes and feel something click.

But the truth is, I don't even want to try them on.

Because I see what it takes. I see how all-consuming it is. The noise, the messy house, the body changes, the worry, the fatigue, the constant mental load. And I just don't want that life for myself. Even if it comes with cute giggles and cuddles and crayon drawings that say, "*I love you.*"

So no, I'm not a dog person. Or a kid person. I'm a my-own-person person.

And that feels like enough.

Chapter 4

You're Allowed to Love Your Life

"This wasn't the life I planned. It was better."

When I first moved out of Justin's place, I was scared of what I had just walked away from. I didn't know it yet, but I was standing at the beginning of something much better: the version of my life that would be for *me*.

And then I met Margot.

She lived in the apartment above mine. A retired nutritionist in the medical field with the kind of presence you don't forget. Warm but sharp, unshakeable in her beliefs, someone who doesn't take shit from anyone. She had this dry wit and a kind of command that didn't demand attention but earned it the moment she walked into a room.

One day, while we were chatting outside, she casually mentioned she'd never had kids.

Not as a confession. Not as a *"here's the reason"* kind of thing.

Just a statement of fact. No apology. No softening. No edges sanded down to make it easier for other people to hear.

She wasn't ashamed. She didn't hedge.

She was just a badass woman living a successful, meaningful, vibrant life and children had never been part of her equation.

Honestly? I'd never met a woman like that before.

At least not someone who said it out loud.

We got close over the next year. Dinners, long talks, check-ins after hard days. We both loved trying new restaurants and cuisines. And our meals were always paired with deep conversation and, occasionally, an unknowing life lesson or two.

We joke that she was my "apartment mom," and I was her "apartment daughter."

And in those fragile months, when I was redefining what my womanhood, adulthood, and my future looked like, she really was that for me.

She reminded me, not through lectures or advice, but just by existing, that a woman's success has never belonged to one storyline.

Watching her thrive in her 70s, still traveling, still curious, still yelling at the TV when the San Francisco Giants did something great or something dumb, still unapologetically herself. It felt like witnessing my own future through a cracked door.

Before I met her, I thought success looked like marriage, a baby, a mortgage.

I thought it looked like a chaotic fridge covered in preschool artwork and calendar reminders for dance recitals.

But with Margot, I saw a new kind of success.

Stillness. Autonomy. A porch you can sit on without being interrupted every two seconds. Enough energy at the end of the day to actually enjoy your life.

And peace. So much peace.

I realized I wasn't alone in that discovery. Katherine, a woman I interviewed while writing this book, had a similar moment. In her early 20s, she befriended an older woman who lived the kind of bold, joyful life that stops you in your tracks. Weeknight theater outings, weekend dog sledding trips, hobbies like ballet started at forty.

She was magnetic. Adventurous. Unapologetically childfree.

Katherine told me:

"She made me realize that having children was actually a choice. I realized that the question we'd always asked each other when we were younger was, 'How many kids do you want?' Not, 'Do you want kids?'"

That one moment reframed everything for her.

Katherine eventually had her own clarity during her teacher training, while observing a group of students.

"They were lovely kids," she said. *"Normal, happy teenagers. But all I could think was: I don't want one of them in my house. I don't want to come home to that or be responsible for it."*

She adores her students. Finds them hilarious, even rewarding. She loves babies too, but only until about eight months, when they stop being cute blobs and start becoming loud, mobile chaos machines.

She's close with her family. Loves her nieces and nephews. But she's never felt particularly drawn to children.

"I adore teaching," she told me. *"But I also love coming home to my quiet, childfree house."*

Katherine, like Margot, built a life she loves.

One full of meaning, movement, hobbies, art, deep friendships, and ridiculously pampered cats.

She told me she often thinks of that woman she met in her 20s, the one who cracked the door open for her, and hopes she's become that person for someone else now.

When her students ask if she has kids, she tells the truth. She explains why she chose not to.

And sometimes, she sees it. That look. The one that says, *"Wait...I didn't know that was allowed."*

That look has stayed with me too.

Because for a long time, I didn't know either.

I didn't know a woman could have a satisfying, love-filled, meaningful life without kids. Or be complete without handing her days over to someone else's needs. I didn't know that joy, freedom, contribution, and legacy could come in other forms.

But now I see it everywhere.

Courtney, one of my best friends who you'll get to know more about later, is always hiking or skiing or camping. Living big and uncontained.

My former coworker Helga and her husband are always off somewhere new. Another country, another national park, another bucket-list adventure.

Margot still travels, even in her 70s, savoring every season and experience with intention.

And me?

I have a career I care deeply about. A home I've built with love.

Friends I trust. Cats I adore. And a quiet I treasure.

I fall asleep when I'm tired, read books without interruption, rearrange furniture for no reason, and wake up naturally to nothing but silence.

No one asks me to cut their food into tiny pieces. No one interrupts me in the bathroom. No one depends on me for everything, every day. *(Though real talk? I have just described my cats.)*

And maybe that sounds small to some people. But to me, it's everything.

There are so many ways to love your life.

There are so many different kinds of full.

And you don't need to defend yours or explain it to anyone.

You're allowed to love your life, exactly as it is.

Even if it doesn't include children.

Even if it doesn't look like what anyone expected.

Even if it took you years, or decades, or a woman upstairs with a fierce attitude and a home office instead of a guest room to remind you that you get to choose your own version of enough.

Chapter 5
Birthing Something Else

"Motherhood isn't the only thing worth creating."

There's a reason we use the word *"birth"* when we talk about bringing something important into the world.

Birth is effort. It's labor. It's raw, vulnerable, and life-altering.

But it doesn't always have to involve a child.

For some women, that birth is literal and beautiful. But for others, like me, the things we bring into the world look different.

I didn't birth a baby. I built a career I care deeply about, created a home that gives me peace, and nurtured relationships full of truth, joy, and absurd inside jokes.

We don't talk enough about the other things women create when they're not creating children. The businesses. The art. The books. The support systems. The personal revolutions. The healing. The wild bird sanctuaries we build in our backyards.

Yes, that last one's mine.

During my breakup with Justin, that apartment became my soft landing. The place where I cried, rebuilt, and rediscovered who I was without someone else in the picture.

But after a year, something shifted. I had outgrown it. Not just the apartment itself *(though more counter space wouldn't have hurt)*, but the version of myself who first walked through that door.

I was no longer unraveling on the bathroom floor. I was someone steadier. Softer. Braver.

I found a small house on the same street. Same zip code, whole new chapter. I moved in just before the new year, and something about it felt symbolic, like I was finally stepping into a life that fit.

And from there? I started building.

Not a nursery. Not a family tree.

But a backyard filled with life.

Solar lights, fountains, suet feeders, a squirrel deterrent that doesn't work. Before I knew it, I had finches and chickadees and towhees and doves and more visiting daily, each one with their own little rhythm. I learned their sounds. I watched them nest in trees I didn't plant but now feel oddly protective of. I researched more plants and shrubs they would like and planted those too.

I built a space that made me feel safe and alive. I planted herbs I had never used before. I bought yard décor I didn't need but deeply wanted.

I had created something. Not for the sake of anyone else's joy, but for mine. It's become my peace. And it's actually where I wrote most of this book.

That yard didn't exist before I chose it.

And it has brought me back to myself more times than I can count.

When I say women birth other things, I don't mean we're just keeping busy or compensating for not having children. These creations are not a backup plan. They are meaningful. They are real.

Some people birth children.
Some people birth art.
Some people birth healing.

Some of us create spaces so safe and sacred that even a hooded oriole feels welcome.

And some of us build careers that never make headlines but still leave people better than we found them.

I work for a nonprofit that supports families and clinicians who provide care to people with autism and intellectual/developmental disabilities. It's not glamorous. But it matters.

I've helped build and shape a training platform that equips thousands of clinicians to do their work with more knowledge, more clarity, and more impact. I've streamlined programs, restructured systems, and helped create continuing education pathways for people who give everything to others.

No one's handing me a Mother's Day card for that.

But it's still labor.

It's still a form of nurturing.

It's still something I helped build from nothing into something that helps others thrive.

Some days, it's exhausting. All days, it's beautiful. I wouldn't trade it for the world.

We don't talk enough about the emotional and creative effort women give to things that don't fit in a stroller.

When people talk about fulfillment, they often mean it in a maternal sense. The baby in your arms; the family around your table; the matching pajamas at Christmas.

That's beautiful. For the people who want it.

But it's not the only version of a full life.

There are women who give birth to change.

To movements. To businesses. To late-in-life reinventions.

To a new version of themselves they fought like hell to find.

There are women who pour their love into things that don't cry at night but still make the world softer and better.

And if you've ever worried that you're missing out on life's "greatest joy," let me offer you another version of joy.

The moment you walk into your quiet, cat-filled home and feel peace instead of panic.

The sound of birds in the morning and knowing they trust you enough to return each day.

The text from a friend that says, *"Thank you for making me feel seen today."*

The kind of Friday night where no one needs you but your couch, your wine, and your Netflix.

The day your work quietly changes someone's life and they don't even know your name.

This is the kind of joy that doesn't scream. It doesn't come with balloons or gender reveals.

It's not always photogenic.

But it's yours. And it's enough.

It took me a long time to stop measuring my life by what I hadn't created and start recognizing everything I had.

So no, I haven't given birth.

But I've nurtured growth.
I've cultivated safety.
I've built something beautiful.

And I birthed this book. Through emotional labor, grief labor, and truth-telling labor. The kind that stretches you *(without needing stitches afterward)*, the kind that shows you who you really are.

I hope you create something you love.
I hope you tend to something that brings you peace.
I hope you recognize the labor you've already done.

The invisible kind, the creative kind, the kind no one celebrates.

Because motherhood isn't the only way we bring things into the world. The proof is everywhere. Women who lived on their own terms. Women who gave the world something lasting.

And we're in damn good company.

Dolly Parton built a global literacy empire through her Imagination Library.

Oprah Winfrey created a media legacy and a school for girls in South Africa.

Virginia Woolf gave us words and wonder.

Ricki Lake shared her truth and made space for others.

Greta Garbo chose solitude and autonomy over expectation.

Jane Austen gave the world novels still taught centuries later.

Condoleezza Rice broke barriers without a family of her own.

Frida Kahlo painted her pain into power.

Coco Chanel changed how women dress and live.

Simone de Beauvoir wrote the feminist blueprint.

Anjelica Huston chose independence.

Kim Cattrall refused to apologize for her choice.

Tracee Ellis Ross said she's not missing a thing and means it.

Jennifer Aniston endured relentless scrutiny and still stood firm.

Gloria Steinem gave a voice to a movement.

Queen Elizabeth I ruled an empire alone and unapologetically.

Ashley Judd turned her focus to activism and global change.

Helen Mirren has said she has 'no maternal instinct whatsoever.'

Betty White gave us decades of laughter and advocacy.

None of these women had children.

All of them birthed something extraordinary.

Section Two: BINGO!

Have you ever had a conversation where you said you didn't want kids and instantly regretted being honest?

Not because you were unsure.

But because you knew what was coming next.

The look of pity. The head tilt. The script.

"You'll change your mind."
"You just haven't met the right person."
"You're too young to know."
"But you'd be such a good mom."

That script? That's called getting "Bingoed".

It's what happens when people respond to your childfree decision with cliché after cliché, assuming their ignorance of your decision trumps your clarity.

Often they mean well. Sometimes they're trying to win a one-sided debate.

Either way, the message underneath is the same:

"You're just confused and couldn't possibly know what's best for your own life if that's your stance."

Childfree Bingo. One square for every judgment, guilt trip, or backhanded compliment we've heard a thousand times before. But the center square? That's the one that matters most: IT'S YOUR FUCKING LIFE.

But this isn't just a game. It's a pattern.

And like all patterns, it starts to wear on you.

That's why this section exists.

To validate.

To call out the scripts we're tired of hearing.

To offer the words maybe you wish you had been equipped with during an awkward exchange.

To remind you that if you've ever sat there blinking in disbelief after being Bingoed that you're not alone.

So grab your Bingo card.

Write down the prize you will treat yourself to after you "win" for enduring all the silly comments.

Mark off the squares.

And know that every time you've heard one of these lines, you've stood your ground, even if you didn't have the perfect words at the time.

Now, you do.

Childfree Bingo

Color in each phrase when you hear it.
Gift yourself a reward when you complete the board!

My
Reward: _____

"It's the most important job."	"But it's so rewarding!"	"You'll change your mind."	"Someday you'll want to settle down."	"But what will you do with your life?"
"You're just selfish."	"It's different when they're your own."	"How many cats do you have?"	"When will we get grandkids?"	"It will be worth it."
"Don't you want to leave a legacy?"	"Don't you want a family?"	IT'S YOUR FUCKING LIFE!!!	"Your clock will start ticking eventually."	"Must be nice to have all that free time."
"You're missing out on life's greatest joy."	"Aren't you curious to see what they'd look like?"	"Have you considered adoption?"	"But who will take care of you when you're old?"	"What about your family name?"
"What if your kid cures cancer?"	"You're still so young!"	"You just haven't met the right man."	"You'll regret it someday."	"You'd be such a good mom."

Chapter 6

Things People Say

We've all heard them. Sometimes with a condescending grin. Sometimes from people who genuinely mean well. But no matter how it's delivered, it usually lands the same:

Like doubt disguised as curiosity.
Like judgment wrapped in a compliment.
Like "I know you better than you know yourself."

Let's break down the greatest hits of Childfree Bingo and what they really mean.

"You'll Change Your Mind"

Translation: *"I don't believe you."*

This is the classic. It shows up early and often, usually when you're just starting to find your footing. Sometimes it's said with a smirk. Other times with pity. Either way, it's meant to undermine your clarity.

Someone I interviewed while writing this book, Natalie, said:

"People kept saying, 'You'll change your mind,' and I believed them. So, I kept waiting...and the only thing that changed was my confidence. Not my desire."

Some people do change their minds. That's allowed.

But assuming we will isn't support. It's dismissal.

"Your Clock Just Hasn't Started Ticking Yet"

For some of us, the only alarm that's gone off lately is our birth control reminders.

Sure, hormones are real. Clocks tick. Bodies change.

But not every woman hears the same ticking.

When I interviewed Ava, she told me:

"As a young adult, I wondered when my biological clock would start ticking and my aversion to pregnancy would wane, like my friends'. It never has."

For Kayla, someone else I interviewed, it was similar:

"I would try to envision the stereotypical life. The big house, yard, kids, etc. But no matter how hard I tried, the visions came up blank."

Hormones aren't homing beacons.

If there's no internal ticking, maybe it's just peace.

"You Just Haven't Met the Right Person Yet"

If only it were that simple. I don't need to meet the right person to suddenly undo what I know about myself.

This isn't a Disney movie. I'm not waiting for someone to show up and flip the maternal switch while I stand in a meadow wondering why my ovaries won't burst into song.

"You'd Be Such a Good Mom"

Thank you. I probably would.

But being good at something doesn't mean you want to do it.

I'd probably be good at running a business. Or hosting a podcast. Or law school.

Doesn't mean I want to build my whole life around any of those things.

Aptitude does not equal obligation.

Amanda put it perfectly:

"You're seen as a broodmare that hasn't used your full potential by refusing to reproduce."

As if everything we are, our empathy, our steadiness, our softness, our strength, is only valuable when funneled toward raising a child.

As if not using those traits to mother means we've wasted them entirely.

You know what I do mother?

I mother my team at work. I protect them, advocate for them, stay late for them, take hits for them, step in when they're stretched too thin.

I mother my cats. To a truly absurd degree. I schedule their vet visits. I monitor their food and hydration. I've rearranged my entire home to accommodate their comfort and, no lie, eight cat towers *(I know...)*.

I mother the people I love.

I'm the one who checks in, remembers the important dates, sends care packages.

The one who shows up when the group text gets hit with *"We just broke up and I don't want to be alone right now."* The one my friend Courtney asks to be her checkpoint for her solo hiking excursions so I can call Search and Rescue if I have not heard from her by a certain point.

Maternal instincts and children are not mutually exclusive.

"You'll Regret It Someday"

Regret is the boogeyman of the childfree life. People love to dangle it in front of us like a cautionary tale:

"You say that now…but just wait until you're older and alone and sobbing into your microwave dinner on Mother's Day."

Regret is real. But so is acceptance.

Everything in life comes with trade-offs. Every decision means closing one door and walking through another.

Besides, regret isn't just for those who are childfree.

There are people who regret becoming parents.

There are parents who love their kids deeply and still mourn the version of themselves that got buried under the demands and expectations of motherhood.

So, if regret is part of the deal either way, then it's not a threat. It's a risk.

And risk is part of every choice we make.

As Ava told me:

"I might regret not having kids someday. But I know I'd regret having them right now."

Maybe regret isn't the scariest possibility.

Maybe it's resentment.

Also: I trust my future self.

She's going to love the naps.

"You're Missing Out on Life's Greatest Joy"

Nope. I'm just choosing a different version of it.

Mine looks like:

Peaceful mornings
Wine in the bathtub
Birdwatching
Having time to write this book

My greatest joys might not be yours. And that's the point. We all have our own idea of what it looks like.

"It's Different When They're Yours"

Sure. But different doesn't necessarily mean better.

Different might mean louder, messier, more expensive.

As if the feelings I have around overstimulation, exhaustion, and anxiety will just vanish once I see my baby's face. Like my entire nervous system will reset when I see a tiny version of myself.

Yes, women do change during and after pregnancy.

They experience dramatic shifts in estrogen, progesterone, prolactin, and cortisol, all of which can cause mood swings and fatigue, and contribute to postpartum depression.

I'm good off all that.

I wouldn't buy a house hoping I might grow to love it.

I wouldn't take a job assuming I'll probably enjoy it eventually.

So why would I create a human on the gamble that I'll feel differently once it's mine?

I'm not willing to bet my life, or someone else's, on that.

"But Who Will Take Care of You When You're Old?"

Probably a private nurse I hire named Linda.

Having a child isn't a long-term care policy.

It's not a guarantee. It's not a transaction.

And frankly, that burden shouldn't be placed on anyone.

What if that kid grows up and can't help you?
What if they won't?
What if they do, but it breaks them in the process?

So, if the worst-case scenario is me living in a cozy apartment I own at 85, watching Chopped reruns with a couple of cats and Linda, I'm doing great.

"What If Your Kid Cures Cancer?"

And what if they don't?

Honestly, my kid would be more likely to inherit my autoimmune diseases, severely debilitating anxiety, maybe some of my OCD, or one of the other mental health conditions that has plagued my family than they would go on to cure cancer. I already know what it is like to live with that all and I would not wish that upon anyone. Let alone create it.

"But Don't Your Parents Want Grandkids?"

Probably. But they also want me to be happy.

Like many of the other Bingos, this one often comes from a genuine place, especially when it's a parent asking.

But that doesn't make it any less painful.

A woman I interviewed named Olivia told me:

"My dad, who is the best person ever, once asked if my lack of wanting kids was because of something they did or didn't do as parents. That hurt me deeply."

I'm lucky. I've never felt that kind of pressure from my parents.

But I've definitely put that pressure on myself.

This was one of the hardest parts of choosing to be childfree.

My dad loves kids. His entire career was spent building youth sports programs, the kind designed to give kids their first taste of the game, and to help them love it. He coached all of my teams growing up, every season, every sport. He had a gift for it. He could get through to the kids while also managing the parents, which in a town like Orinda was no small feat. It's a fiercely competitive town, full of kids bound for club teams and collegiate success. But my dad's focus was different. He cared just as much about the kid who dreaded practice as the one dreaming of a scholarship.

I can still see him on the sidelines, reminding me to pass the ball to the smallest girl on my team instead of taking the shot myself. I was competitive and athletically gifted. I wanted to win, and he knew I could make every shot and win every game. But he wanted everyone on the team to feel that feeling of belonging. He wanted everyone to leave with a positive memory of the game.

He also had this knack for handling the *other* side of youth sports. The parents. When someone would get heated over a bad call, my dad would step in and diffuse it. He'd remind them, gently but firmly, that this was recreational, and that their kids were eight years old. His perspective kept things grounded.

That's what he gave to all of us. The lesson that sports weren't just about winning. They were about kids having fun and leaving with something positive to carry with them. I still have the article from the newspaper that was written about him when he retired. He impacted so many children's lives and left a lasting impression on an entire community.

These days, he's a crossing guard at an elementary school in his retirement, greeting kids by name, high-fiving them as they head into class, keeping them safe on their way home. Last year, the district named him Crossing Guard of the Year. He gets to pour his humor, patience, and energy into a community of kids who light up when they see him.

He would've been the best grandfather and I will always feel an aching remorse that I never got to see him play with my children.

I still really hope my brother has kids someday so my dad can experience the joy and bust out the silliness in the role he was born to play, but I also know he's already found a meaningful way to connect with and care for children.

For other people, this question hits harder, especially when it stirs up trauma.

A lot of women I spoke to cited their difficult or painful upbringings as part of the reason they didn't want to have children themselves.

So, when someone asks about grandkids, it can feel like a gut punch. A reminder of what they've worked so hard to heal from.

But here's the truth: you don't owe your parents a second childhood just because they gave you one.

Your life isn't a group project.

Some parents grieve that dream.

Some are just proud you made an honest choice.

Either way, their dream doesn't get to override your reality.

To Summarize

You don't owe anyone an explanation.

Not for your body. Not for your peace. Not for your joy.

These scripts aren't truths.

They're projections.
They're habits.
They're echoes of what people have been told to say.

You're not un-nurturing. Or confused. Or off-track.

You're just not playing the game.

So, mark the square. Roll your eyes. Yell BINGO!

And remember, the center square's the only one that matters:
it's your fucking life.

Chapter 7

What We Say Back

After a while, the same comments start to feel like reruns. But every now and then, you find yourself wanting to answer back. Not to convince anyone. Just to remind yourself you can.

You want to push back.
You want to educate.
You want to walk away feeling clear, not cornered.

This chapter is for that.

These aren't scripts, they're starting points.

Some are gentle. Some are spicy. Some are just a raised eyebrow and a long sip of wine.

Pick your tone. Pick your peace.

When You Want to Keep It Simple

- "I've thought about it a lot. And my answer is no."

- "I know myself. This just isn't something I want."

- "I don't feel the need to explain my decision."

Sometimes the quietest response is the strongest.

When You're Feeling Diplomatic

- "I'd rather be honest now than risk resentment later."

- "Being a parent is a full-time commitment, and I only want to do it if I feel called to it."

- "There are many ways to live a meaningful life. Parenthood's just one."

Let your calm be contagious. Or deeply unsettling. Either works.

When You're Feeling Bold

- "I did change my mind. I used to think I had to want it. Now I know I don't."

- "I trust myself more than I trust social pressure."

- "If I had a dollar for every time I've heard that, I could afford the child you think I should have."

Bonus points for a confident smile.

When You're Over It

- "Personal decision."

- "I'm good."

- "That's not something I'm discussing today."

- [Raises eyebrow. Sips drink. Changes subject.]

Let your silence be loud.

When You're Inspired by Your Pet

- "I already have kids. They're just covered in fur."

- "I'm raising two cats, a career, and my standards. That's plenty."

- "My dog is happier without kids in the house."

Save these for the folks who you know hate people referring to their pets as children.

When You're Speaking to Someone Who Matters

Sometimes the question comes from someone you love. Someone who's trying but doesn't understand. Here's how you can keep your power and your compassion:

- "This wasn't an easy decision for me. It came with grief. But it also came with clarity."

- "It's not that I don't believe in parenting. It's that I believe in being honest with myself."

- "This choice wasn't made lightly. And I'm proud of it."

- "Thank you for supporting me."

You don't owe them everything. You're not required to educate anyone. But you can let them see your heart.

When You're Talking to Yourself

Sometimes the pressure doesn't come from others. It comes from inside you. From years of expectations. From culture. From silence. In those moments, here's what I hope you say to yourself:

- "I know who I am."

- "I don't have to prove my worth through motherhood."

- "I'm allowed to love my life exactly as it is."

- "My 'no' is not a wound. It's a boundary."

- "I didn't opt out of something. I chose something else."

Say what you need to say. Or don't.

But if you want to, now you've got the words.

And if you forget them, don't worry.

You're still living your truth. Beautifully. Unapologetically.

Even in silence you're still saying it.

I THOUGHT ABOUT IT, AND NO.

It's your fucking life.

Chapter 8

What We Wish People Knew

Being childfree isn't one universal experience.

Sometimes it's deafening. Sometimes it's quiet.

Sometimes it's crystal clear. Sometimes it's layered with confusion.

Sometimes it's freeing. Sometimes it's laced with grief.

Sometimes it's something you don't even say out loud until someone else does first.

I asked other women, and myself, what we most wish people understood about this decision.

Not because we owe anyone an explanation, but because sometimes truth is easier to hear when it comes in many voices.

Here's what we said.

It's Valid — Full stop

"That it's valid, and there's nothing wrong with it. Just 'no, I don't want to' is enough."

— Amanda (37)

"That it's MINE and mine alone. My choices do not in any way impact you at all."

— Olivia (48)

"After years of comparing myself to others and feeling like I was inferior because I never really followed the so-called 'normal' path in life, I've finally accepted that for me, this IS normal."

— Bonnie (44)

Please Stop Making It a Debate

"The decisions of childfree people have absolutely no bearing on how you live your life, so please leave us alone. Stop interrogating us. Stop asking personal, invasive questions. Stop assuming we'll change our minds. Please just say 'Oh, okay,' and move on."

— Emma (45)

"Women should be encouraged to have their own identities separate from being a mom. A woman's purpose in life is not shackled to childbearing."

— Helga (32)

We Thought About It More Than You Think

"I've never really been drawn to kids. The thought of having them felt synonymous with my life being over. People call it selfish, but I think it's the opposite. I know I'm not willing to be the kind of parent a kid deserves, so I choose not to risk harming a child."

— Courtney (32)

"What I wish more people understood is actually quite simple: I've never had the desire to become a parent. You often hear women talk about dreaming of the white picket fence and three kids running around. To me, that sounds like a nightmare. I also know that my upbringing likely shaped this choice. The negative experiences from my childhood stick with me. That's why I try every day to be the kind of person I needed back then — but I only have the energy to share that version of myself with a partner and close friends, not children."

— Casey (36)

And For Me?

This wasn't the easiest decision I've ever made.

I had to weigh serious considerations about my health, my energy, and the kind of life I was capable of giving a child.

I've been called selfish more times than I can count for making this choice.

I didn't want to pass down a body that hurts all the time. A mind that spirals without warning. A set of challenges I didn't choose and wouldn't wish on anyone.

Choosing not to have children was how I broke the cycle.

So, if you ever feel tempted to comment on someone's childfree choice, pause.

You have no idea what they've carried to arrive at that decision.

Be kind. Be curious, if invited. But mostly? Just listen.

What We're Saying

There's no single way to be childfree.

No perfect way to explain it.

And honestly? We shouldn't have to.

But if you've ever wondered what it looks like from the inside, this is it.

We're not lost.
We're not confused.
We're not incomplete.

We're choosing lives that feel honest to us even if they look different from yours.

Section Three:
Big Picture, Big Decisions

This is where things get a little heavier.

Up to now, we've danced around the question. Poked at it, sat with it, maybe even laughed through some of it.

But this next part?

We're going in.

We'll look at the bigger forces that shape our decisions: the world, our bodies, our relationships, our pasts, and the futures we imagine.

Some of it will feel light. Some of it will hit a nerve. All of it matters.

So, take a deep breath.

Whatever brought you to this book, you belong here.

This is a safe space.

And one of the promises I made while writing it was that no uncomfortable, sad, shameful, or scary truth would be too much to name.

So, let's dive in one truth at a time.

Chapter 9

I'd Love to Be a Dad

"Somewhere, there's a dad anthem waiting to be written: 'Dads Just Want to Have Fun'. Think Cyndi Lauper's hit, but instead of 'Best New Artist', it wins a participation trophy."

There's something I've said half-jokingly for years, even before I fully owned my choice to be childfree:

"I would totally have kids if I got to be the dad."

The one who doesn't carry the pregnancy. The one who doesn't have to worry about postpartum depression. The one who isn't expected to breastfeed, run the household, and keep everyone alive and emotionally regulated at all times with a smile.

It's not that dads don't do anything. The good ones show up, big time. But let's be honest, the baseline for moms is so much higher. And heavier.

For a lot of women, motherhood isn't just something they do. It becomes who they are. The identity shift is instant and all-consuming. And if they struggle with it or need a break, society treats it like a personal failure.

Hannah, a woman I spoke to for this book, captured it perfectly:

"It seems like for most parents, especially mothers, kids take up your WHOLE life. It should be your passion, your purpose, not just 'something you do.' I also hated hearing about the unequal parenting expectations between men and women. At some point I thought, 'Being a dad wouldn't be so bad. But no way I'd survive a month as a mom.' Unfortunately, I'm a straight woman, so the dad role is unavailable to me."

I laughed when I first heard that. Because I have had that exact same thought. And I'm sure you may have too. Like, yeah, I'd totally do this...if I got the version with less expectation and way less pressure.

And it's not just a vibe, it's documented.

A 2023 Pew Research Center study found that in opposite-gender partnerships, 70% of moms say they manage their kids' schedules and activities. Nearly three-quarters of moms also say they handle the majority of household responsibilities, even when both parents work full-time.

Another report by Oxfam and the Institute for Women's Policy Research estimates that unpaid caregiving work performed by women in the U.S. would be worth over $1.5 trillion annually if it were compensated.

And here's the kicker: a separate study by Pew Research Center in 2021 reported that 63% of fathers say parenting duties are shared equally with their partner, while only 43% of mothers agree.

So yeah. The math isn't mathing.

Moms are more likely to wake up with the baby, schedule the dentist appointments, remember the birthdays, pack the lunches, soothe the tantrums, and clean up the mess. They're the default.

And "default" isn't just a role. It's a burden.

Even amazing dads, the ones who do their share, still benefit from what I like to call dad privilege.

They're applauded for helping. Moms are expected to perform flawlessly, without rest or resentment.

There's also this bizarre cultural idea that a good woman should want to be consumed by motherhood. That anything less than full devotion is a red flag. If a mom says she needs space or doesn't feel fulfilled, we act like something is wrong with her, not the system.

No one expects fatherhood to become a man's entire personality. But with mothers? It's practically a requirement.

One of my exes, Shawn, once told me he's secretly relieved to be a divorced dad.

He loves his son more than life itself, but he's honest about how consuming parenting is.

Sharing custody means he gets to have half his life to himself, and honestly, that logic tracks.

My frustration isn't with fathers themselves. It's with the system that rewards them for doing the bare minimum while punishing moms for doing anything less than everything.

It's the double standard. The lopsided praise. The way we assign worth based on gendered expectations instead of effort or intent.

And before anyone thinks I'm anti-dad, let me be clear: I love dads. Especially mine.

My dad was the maternal parent in my life. My mom loved me, and I have sweet memories of her with our late-night cuddles, watching 90210 together when I was a kid and sushi lunches now that I am an adult, but my dad was the one who took on most of the daily caretaking. He remembered to feed us, coached my sports teams, quizzed me on spelling as he drove me to school, and asked all about my day as he drove me home. He was both Mom and Dad when he needed to be, and he did it all without ever making it seem like a burden.

Later, in my 20s and 30s, when I'd talk to him about having kids someday, he'd just smile, tilt his head a little, and say with a wink:

"Cats are great."

He never pushed. Never pressured. Just reminded me, in his quiet way, that a full, loving life doesn't have to follow one script.

And damned if he wasn't right.

Chapter 10

Frozen in Time

"To freeze, or not to freeze…"

My company offers a fertility care benefit to all employees, something that's genuinely progressive and generous, especially in the nonprofit space. When I first heard about it, I did something I never thought I would:

I signed up.

Not because I was actively trying to preserve my fertility, but because I wanted to understand what my options were.

My mom had brought up egg freezing to me more than once in my late 20s and early 30s. It was usually framed gently, as a way to keep the door open in case I changed my mind later. She wasn't pressuring me. I think she just wanted to make sure I had all the information. Her background in OBGYN clinics always opened the door for these kinds of discussions and access to knowledge, birth control, really anything a young woman would need. And I am so grateful I had that presence in my life.

So, when the benefit became available at work, I figured: Why not just explore it?

By that point, though, I was already in my early 30s. And even though that's not "old," I assumed the window of opportunity for ideal results had already started closing.

Still, I looked into it. And I'm really glad I did, even if I chose not to move forward.

The Stats Behind the Storage

Egg freezing has become much more common and for good reason. It offers a kind of reproductive backup plan, especially helpful for people who aren't sure they want kids yet, are waiting for the right partner, or are undergoing medical treatments that could affect fertility.

In the U.S., roughly 1 in 5 large employers now offer coverage for egg freezing through insurance or fertility benefits. It's still far from universal, but the number is rising, and so is demand.

But like most things in the reproductive space, it's not as simple as it sounds.

Timing matters. A lot.

Success rates for retrieving and storing healthy eggs drop significantly with age. Here's a general snapshot of what fertility specialists estimate your odds might be of freezing enough viable eggs for a potential future pregnancy:

•Under age 34: About a 74% chance of retrieving enough healthy eggs

•Ages 35 to 37: Drops to 55%

•Ages 38 to 40: Falls further to 18%

•Ages 41 to 42: Just 2%

These numbers aren't meant to scare anyone, but rather to highlight why the process can feel like a race against time. And like many things tied to women's health, there's pressure baked into the language: *"Don't wait too long."*, "You better d*ecide soon."*, *"Your eggs won't wait."*

Even the name, *egg freezing*, carries a subtle urgency. You're literally trying to preserve them before they expire.

I 100% Support It — But It Wasn't for Me

I think fertility preservation is a powerful tool, especially for those who might want kids eventually but aren't ready right now.

If that's you, and you have the access, support, or means, I strongly encourage you to look into it.

Having options can be empowering.

So can choosing not to pursue them.

I didn't freeze my eggs. Not because I didn't think the benefit was valuable, but because I didn't feel that nudge in my gut to do it. I wasn't putting off motherhood because I was unsure or overwhelmed or waiting for the right time. I had already started to feel that "no" taking shape, slowly, quietly, but steadily.

Egg freezing just helped me confirm it.

It helped me realize I wasn't afraid of running out of time.

I was relieved not to be racing it.

Chapter 11

The Price Tag of Parenthood

"Single with no dependents" is apparently considered a "luxury tax."

There's this thing people say when you mention the cost of raising kids:

"You can't put a price on love."

Cool. Well, LendingTree did.

A 2025 study found that the average annual cost of raising a child in the United States had climbed 35.7% since they last conducted this study in 2023, bringing the total cost per child to a whopping $297,674 over 18 years.

That is, quite literally, more than the cost of buying a home outright in 23 states, a luxury vehicle, or even a Birkin bag.

But wait, there's more.

A 2025 LendingTree update reported that the average American parent spends 22.6% of their income on child-rearing costs each year. That's not just a budgeting challenge. That's financial strain baked into the system.

And yet, no one talks about this. Not seriously, anyway.

We're all supposed to just nod along and pretend that dropping over a quarter of a million dollars (again — per child) is just "part of life."

Something you'll figure out.
Something that's always worth it.
Something you'll "make work."

Honestly? The math alone could've been my birth control.

Where All That Money Goes

I looked into the results of income spent on children. And it was bleak.

•**Housing (29%)**
Kids need space. Whether that means upgrading to a bigger place or moving to a pricier ZIP code to get into a "good" school district. Either way, you're paying for square footage and access.

•**Food (18%)**
They grow. They snack. They decide they hate the thing they loved yesterday.

•**Childcare (16%)**
If both parents work, and most do, childcare becomes a second mortgage. In many states, it runs $10K–$17K per year, and in

urban centers, even more. That's before after-school programs or summer care.

•**Extracurriculars (remaining 37%)** Think: soccer leagues, piano lessons, art classes, swim team, or $300 ballet costumes they wear once. Also, health insurance, medical copays, school supplies, winter coats, birthday party invites, summer camps, lost water bottles, screen-time guilt toys, and yes, more snacks.

And it's not just the U.S.

Globally, the rising cost of raising children is triggering similar conversations and concerns.

In South Korea, the estimated cost of raising one child is now nearly eight times the average income. While housing is the biggest expense in the U.S., in Korea it's education. Many families turn to costly private academies to supplement what they see as insufficient public schooling. In 2022 alone, Korean households spent nearly $20 billion on private education, with an average of nearly $400 per month per child going toward extra tutoring and classes.

China isn't far behind, with the cost of child-rearing coming in at around seven times the country's per capita income. Though absolute costs may appear lower than in the U.S., the financial strain is steep when compared to average wages, a burden that's contributing to record low birth rates. Both countries are now seeing social and economic ripple effects as fewer families feel they can afford to have children at all.

In other words: this isn't just a personal decision. It's a global one. And many people, from Seoul to Sacramento, are arriving at the same conclusion:

It's just too expensive.

Some families meticulously budget for all of this.

Some just white-knuckle it.

Either way, it adds up fast.

And it's not like the government's stepping in to cover the Costco-size cartons of formula.

...Or are they?

Reproducing: America's Favorite Tax Strategy

Here's what you might get if you decide to have a kid:

•Up to $2,000 per child via the Child Tax Credit

•A larger standard deduction

•Head of household filing status

•Dependent deductions

•State-level benefits like childcare credits, child savings account contributions, or free preschool (depending on how baby-happy your legislature is feeling)

Is it helpful? Sure.

But also...it's kind of weird.

When I think of tax write-offs, I think, charitable donations, business expenses, hell, even gambling losses.

Not creating a human.

Meanwhile, in Childfree Land...

It's like paying a premium for your peace and quiet.

•No deductions.

•No dependent credits.

•No sweet state perks.

Just freedom and full price everything.

Still, it's wildly cheaper.

The Bottom Line

We're not really supposed to talk about this part.

It makes you look greedy.

Like you're putting money ahead of love.

Like you're too cold, too calculating, too privileged, or too pessimistic.

But here's the thing:

Money matters.

So does stability.
So does health.
So does joy.

And if the financial, mental, or emotional forecast doesn't look safe for a child, then choosing not to have one isn't selfish.

It's responsible. It's protective. It's loving in a different direction.

I have nothing but respect for people who choose to raise children. But let's not pretend it's simple. Or cheap.

Because this choice has a price tag.

And it's okay to read it before you swipe the card.

Trigger Warning

This next chapter contains sensitive themes including school shootings, climate change, political instability, and suicide. Please take care while reading.

Author's Note:

This chapter is not meant to be politically charged.

It's not about left or right or trying to divide anyone.

It's about real fears, real risks, and the real world we'd be handing to future children.

For many of us, these aren't headlines. They're the daily backdrop to life.

This chapter reflects the current state of things and how it helped shape my decision.

Chapter 12
The World I'd Be Brining Them Into

"It's not fear-mongering. It's reality."

Remember how I said I would have loved to have been a dad? Well, I also would've loved to be a mom in the 90s.

But today?

Raising a child through active shooter drills?

Explaining why the sky is orange from wildfire smoke?

Reassuring them when the Supreme Court undoes another basic right?

Because that's the world I'd be bringing them into.

And no matter how loving, stable, or prepared I might be, I can't insulate a child from all that.

I could give them a bedtime story and a warm dinner, sure.

But I couldn't guarantee clean air. Or safe schools. Or bodily autonomy.

And it breaks my heart that we have to weigh that.

School Shootings

In the United States, school shootings have become tragically common. A 2025 CNN report stated that in 2008, there were 18 per year; by 2024, there were 83 per year. And as of July 2025, another 32 have already occurred in the first 7 months of the year. I've seen the arguments. "*Don't let fear stop you from living your life.*"

But this isn't just fear.

It's a conscious, moral reckoning with the world we've made.

Mental Health: The Other Pandemic

Let's say your kid makes it to adulthood. They'll still face the mental health crisis head-on because it's not going away.

The youth mental health crisis isn't just rising. It's surging. And it's showing up younger than ever.

In the United States:

A 2024 NIH study found that suicide rates among preteens (ages 8 to 12) have been increasing by roughly 8% annually since 2008. The sharpest rises were among:

•Female preteens

•Black preteens

•American Indian/Alaska Native, Asian/Pacific Islander, and Hispanic preteens

Black preteens had the highest overall suicide rate, while Hispanic preteens saw the greatest percentage increase.

While still less common than teen suicides, the rate is rising alarmingly fast and showing that suicide is no longer considered a "teen issue" alone.

The Children's Hospital Association reported a 166% increase in ER visits for suicide attempts and self-injury among children ages 5 to 18 between 2016 and 2022, based on their Pediatric Health Information System (PHIS).

Suicide is now the second leading cause of death for U.S. youth ages 10 to 24, accounting for over 6,500 deaths per year.

Globally:

According to the World Health Organization, suicide is the second leading cause of death for children ages 10 to 14, and the fourth leading cause among young adults ages 15 to 29 globally. While data collection remains inconsistent across countries, current estimates suggest that over 700,000 people die by suicide every year, with youth increasingly affected.

The burden is especially severe in lower and middle-income countries, where over 70% of suicides take place. Limited access to mental health care, food scarcity, systemic poverty, and political instability all compound the risk. Countries like Lesotho, Guyana, and Eswatini have among the highest youth suicide rates per capita worldwide.

Additional Global Risk Factors Include:

•**Firearms Access:** In the U.S., over 50% of youth suicides involve guns.

•**Gender and Sexual Identity:** In one U.K. study, 68% of LGBTQIA+ youth reported suicidal thoughts. Rates were even higher among transgender and Black LGBTQIA+ youth. Many cited school-based harassment, bullying, and social exclusion.

•**Chronic Illness and Disability:** Young people with long-term physical or psychiatric conditions are more vulnerable to suicidal ideation, especially when paired with social stigma or lack of support.

•**Abuse and Trauma:** Childhood maltreatment is one of the strongest predictors of suicide risk. Nearly 20% of suicide cases in the U.K. were linked to abuse or neglect.

•**Academic Pressure and Bullying:** In highly competitive cultures, the pressure to succeed can be lethal. More than a quarter of youth suicide cases in the U.K. involved stress around school exams or bullying.

And what do we offer them?

Underfunded school counselors. Insurance policies that don't cover mental health. And an endless cycle of *"have you tried yoga?"* type platitudes instead of real care.

We tell kids to speak up.

But we don't guarantee anyone will listen or be qualified to help.

We're raising children in a world that's louder, scarier, more connected and disconnected at the same time, and our mental health systems are nowhere near equipped to handle it.

Climate Change Isn't Coming. It's Here

My state burns every summer; maybe yours floods.

Like school shootings, natural disasters are no longer shocking, they're expected. Hurricanes, floods, wildfires, tsunamis. These headlines used to stop you in your tracks. Now, they're page two news.

Storms are stronger, seasons are broken, and summers are stretching longer, hotter, and less livable.

Kids born today will live through environmental shifts we still can't fully predict.

Rights Aren't Guaranteed. They're Being Undone

Abortion. Trans rights. Book bans.

Every week there's a new US law that feels like something out of a dystopian novel. Laws that decide whose bodies, identities, and stories are allowed to exist.

What if they're queer?
What if they're disabled?
What if they just want to be themselves?

How do you raise a child to be compassionate, brave, and free when their world feels so fragile?

Kayla told me how the state of the world pushed her to claim autonomy over her own body:

"My current method of protection was an IUD that wouldn't need to be replaced till my mid-30s. The idea of sterilization had floated through my mind, but I figured I'd wait till my next one was up and if I still wanted one then I would get it. Fast forward to the end of 2024, the day after the election, I called my doctor to schedule a sterilization consult. I found a wonderful doctor who heard and respected my decision to be childfree.

Now the real journey begins. I am currently embarking on the most freeing and empowering journey I never knew I needed. When I received the final insurance approval, I broke down sobbing. It felt like a weight had been lifted off my shoulders, one I never knew I was carrying. The looming threat of motherhood had been removed. I finally knew what safety felt like in my own body. I no longer needed to live in fear.

As I sit here and wait for my surgery date, I have a renewed sense of hope and optimism for my future. I can finally envision my life clearly. And I can't wait to see where it takes me."

That's what we mean when we say this isn't about fear.

It's about freedom.

And for a lot of us, freedom means not bringing a child into a world that feels actively hostile to the very things we'd want to protect them from.

One of my friends who you will get to know more about later, Casey, is already sterilized. She's been an incredible resource, not just for me, but for our other friend Courtney, who's considering it too. It's becoming more common in our circle, not because we're afraid of parenting, but because we're afraid of some old white men in power making decisions about our bodies on our behalf.

Bottom Line

I know this is heavy.

It's something I truly hope people are considering. Not to scare them, but to be honest about what this choice really means today.

I know plenty of incredible parents doing their best to raise kind, thoughtful kids in this chaos. I just knew I wasn't built to parent in it.

Chapter 13

Ethically Childfree

"I only have so many spoons."

After looking at the world my future child would inherit, I had to turn inward and look at what I would be able to give them.

Some people don't want kids because they just don't.

Some for lifestyle reasons. Some for freedom.

And then there are those of us who've made the choice not to have children because of a moral consideration of what we might be passing down to our kids, or to the world.

That's where I land.

I identify as ethically childfree. Not because I think it's a superior reason. Not because I think parenthood is a bad choice. But because I believe that, for me, having children would be an irresponsible one.

I want to say clearly: most childfree people I know have wrestled with ethical considerations in some form, even if they don't call themselves that. Whether it's about the climate, the future, finances, mental health, or global injustice, many of us have felt the weight of this choice.

So this label isn't a badge. It's just a way to describe my personal turning point.

And that turning point was my body.

As I mentioned earlier, I was a fence-sitter for most of my life. Some days I thought I wanted to be a mom, other days I felt no strong urge.

But over time, as my health challenges became harder to ignore and the state of the world became impossible to unsee, that fence started to feel less like a place to pause and more like a gate I should close gently behind me.

Being ethically childfree means choosing not to have children based on moral, philosophical, or humanitarian concerns, like overpopulation, instability, or in my case, the potential to pass down physical or mental health conditions.

After everything I laid out in the last chapter, school shootings, climate collapse, political extremism, bringing a child into today's world already feels like a gamble.

But for me, the biggest reason was my body's limitations.

My rheumatoid arthritis has shaped my life in every way. Physically, emotionally, energetically. It's not just some aches or stiffness. It's chronic pain. Constant fatigue. A compromised immune system. I get sick easily. I've developed other conditions just from having RA. My joints are beginning to calcify and deform despite over a decade of pumping my body full of nearly every RA medication that Western medicine has to offer.

They don't even know exactly how RA develops, which means there may be a genetic component. And that's not a risk I could bring myself to take.

The idea that I could pass this down and that I might watch my own child someday struggle with the same pain I've carried was enough to guide the choice for me.

Because the way I would show up for a child wouldn't be my best.

And kids deserve your best.

There's a concept called The Spoon Theory, originally written by Christine Miserandino who struggles with a different autoimmune disease, Lupus. But it applies here, too. It's the idea that people with chronic illness wake up each day with a limited number of "spoons," or units of energy. Every activity from getting dressed, making breakfast, responding to an email, they all cost a spoon.

Most people don't have to think about their energy reserves. I have to ration mine. I only get so many spoons a day. And I've had to learn to spend them wisely.

I use mine to work at a job I love.

I use them to go on runs when I can, or sit outside and feed the birds, or go to trivia nights at local breweries with my friends.

Those things refill my well. They bring me joy. They let me show up for myself and others in meaningful, sustainable ways.

But you can't give from an empty well.

And mine is often empty.

That's not to say raising a child can't be a beautiful or meaningful way to spend one's time. It absolutely is for some people.

People with more spoons.

People whose bodies don't feel like a battlefield most days.

For me, choosing not to have children was about knowing and respecting my limits.

I chose not to have children based on what I can carry, and what I couldn't bear to pass on.

That doesn't mean I never grieve.

Some days, even this clear-eyed decision holds a quiet sadness. But grief doesn't mean regret. It means I took the decision seriously enough to feel everything it asked of me and still chose what I knew was right.

Chapter 14

The Partner Problem

"Maybe I never wanted kids. Maybe I just didn't want to lose the guy who I thought did."

Let's talk about what happens when your dreams aren't entirely your own.

Because for a lot of women, myself included, the question of motherhood doesn't live in isolation. It's tangled up in relationships. In being a "good partner". In making someone else happy. In not losing the person you love.

Sometimes, your answer to *"Do I want kids?"* becomes, *"Well...he does."*

When I was with Shawn, my first long-term partner, we were young. We dated for seven years, and the idea of children was always somewhere in the air, but always in the distant future. I was very close with his family, and since he was their only son, I caught myself romanticizing the idea of giving him a boy to carry on the family name.

Antiquated, I know. But I was in my early 20s, all bright-eyed and bushy-tailed.

Eventually, we broke up. I was 26, and he was the only guy I'd ever dated. Some called it the seven-year itch. For me, it felt more like a slow unraveling. A realization that we were growing in different directions, and I didn't know who I was without him.

A year later I met Justin.

At 2 a.m.
At a dive bar.
I was very drunk.

I walked right up to him, told him he wanted my number, and delivered what I believed was my strongest pickup line in that moment: *"I'm really good at pool."*

(Reader: I am not really good at pool.)

He texted the next day asking to play pool. I had no recollection of meeting him. But we ended up playing later that night and then spending the next six years together.

That relationship was what I call a crossroads relationship.

The one that forces you to ask big questions.

The one where love and pressure blur.

The one that pushes you right up to the edge of who you thought you were.

During those six years, we talked about our future often. We were both in our 30s, and in that window where couples start dreaming out loud. We had baby names picked out. Two boy names, one girl name. I remember thinking we'd probably have two boys but wanted to have my bases covered in case we had a girl. Don't ask me why, it just became part of the imagined life I carried around.

But over time, that version of life stopped feeling like mine.

The relationship itself became toxic. It had never been the healthiest to begin with. *(Hello: I met him while blacked out.)* But it wasn't for lack of love. We truly did care for each other. We just weren't a good fit at that time in our lives.

Looking back, I see how lost I was in those years. I didn't know who I was, so I anchored myself to what I thought he wanted. What I thought were his needs, his goals, his vision of the future.

Being his wife and giving him children became my north star.

Not because I felt deeply called to motherhood, but because I thought that's what gave me value.

That's what would make me enough.

So, when I started quietly wondering if I didn't actually want kids, it felt like I was breaking a sacred contract.

Like I was keeping a secret that could unravel everything.
Like I'd be alone forever.
Like I'd become the lady with seven cats. *(#lifegoals)*

I interviewed a woman named Emma who reminded me of my own early thinking when she said:

"I thought I'd have kids eventually when I was in my teens and early 20s. Not because I actually wanted them, but because that's just what you do, isn't it? You grow up, get married, buy a house, and have kids."

That mindset is hard to unlearn.

My friend Casey finds it nearly impossible to date as a woman who's clear about not wanting kids. The moment she's honest about it, most men either disappear, condescend, or treat her like it's a phase that just hasn't passed yet.

She's not confused.
She's not rebellious.
She just knows herself.

And that shouldn't disqualify her from love.

I remember at one point I started wondering if maybe I was infertile. I'd never been pregnant. Not with Shawn, not with Justin. I was always on birth control, sure, but so were my friends. Plenty of them had "surprises." So, I began to wonder: maybe I just couldn't?

And honestly? Part of me hoped I couldn't.

Because then the decision would be made for me.
Because then I wouldn't have to say it out loud.
Because saying "I don't think I want kids" felt like a betrayal.

Not just to the men I loved, but to the woman I thought I was supposed to become.

There's a particular kind of fear that comes with unraveling your identity in front of someone else, especially when your identity has always been built around the roles you're expected to play.

Partner. Wife. Mom.

So instead of saying it, I sat with it.

Quietly. Lonely. Afraid.

Afraid he wouldn't love me if I told the truth. Afraid no one else ever would, either.

And that's a brutal place to live.

Loving someone and building a life with them while quietly hiding the part of you that's questioning everything.

Turns out, Justin was a fence-sitter too. That helped. But it also made me realize how many of us are walking around performing certainty. Going through the motions. Hoping the desire shows up later.

It's everywhere.

Two years after the Justin breakup, I dipped my toe into the world of online dating. I saw it again and again, this underlying assumption that "childfree" is just a phase. A challenge. A preference you'll change your mind about for the right man.

Shawn, who I have stayed friends with since our breakup, once told me he automatically swipes left on any woman whose profile says, *"Doesn't want children."*

He already had a kid. I laughed and asked him why. His response annoyed me so much. *"It means she's selfish."*

(Clown emoji. Barf emoji. Internal screaming.)

[Yes, the same Shawn who once told me he liked split custody with his ex because it gave him time to himself. But apparently when we want time to ourselves, that's selfish. Cool cool cool.]

Another guy I almost went out with told me, before we had even met, that he "definitely wants kids" but thinks I "seem fun," so he's still "down to meet up."

Weird opener. And it only got worse.

A few days later, he told me my decision to have cats instead of kids was *"fine for now."*

(Clown emoji again. Barf emoji again. Internal screaming intensifies.)

I deleted my account right then and there.

This idea that our "no" is negotiable or incorrect is baked into everything.

Being childfree doesn't mean I'm waiting for someone to change my mind. It also doesn't mean I don't care about anyone but myself.

It means I've thought about it, deeply, painfully, completely, and decided that this is the life that fits.

Fast forward to now, me and Justin are actually back together. Healthier and happier than ever this time though. Older, steadier, and more able to be ourselves. The years apart forced me to get clear on who I am without him, or any man, and I carry that clarity back into the relationship. But here's the thing...being in love again doesn't erase the partner problem. It just reshapes it.

Even now, there are days when I look at him and wonder:

- Does he secretly want something different than me?

- Is he just trying not to hurt my feelings?

- Will he always see me as a temporary chapter instead of a future?

And if I'm being brutally honest, there are still times I wonder:

- Is he the one who will change my mind?

- If it were truly that important to him, would I get on board?

- Would my decision have been different if the circumstances and timing were different?

And that's the partner problem in a nutshell.

When you know who you are but wonder if it's going to cost you the person who feels like home. Or worse, if it's going to cost you the person you chose to be.

Section Four: In Their Words

Not every story in this book is mine.

And that's the point.

The decision to be childfree doesn't come in one shape or one voice.

Sometimes it's certain.
Sometimes it's complicated.
Sometimes it's still unfolding.

This section widens the lens. To show what 'no,' 'maybe, 'or 'not right now' can look like in real life.

Some always knew.
Some changed their minds.
Some are still figuring it out.

They're not here to persuade you.

They're here to share their truth and to remind you that whatever your truth is, it's worth honoring.

You may not see your exact path in theirs.

But you might see your questions, your fears, your hope.

And if not that, maybe just a little relief in knowing you're not alone.

Chapter 15

Courtney's Story - The "Courtney Year" Ick

Meet my friend Courtney. I met her last year on BumbleBFF, and we have been close friends ever since. She used to be a fence sitter. Quietly unsure, slowly unraveling. Her story reminds us that clarity doesn't always strike like lightning. Sometimes it unfolds gently, after loss, after love, after asking hard questions you didn't want the answers to.

"I spent most of my life on the fence. For a long time, I told myself I just wasn't ready yet. That maybe at 28, then 30, then someday, I'd want kids. But the truth is, that moment never came.

I got married young at 21, and for the next decade, I lived in that limbo. My family expected babies. His family expected babies. We bought the house, got the dogs, hit every milestone, and everyone around us just assumed the next one was a kid. That's what you do, right? You get married, and then you have kids.

And I kept thinking, maybe later. Maybe when I feel more settled. Maybe when I'm ready. But I never did.

There was no single 'aha' moment. It was more like a slow unraveling of expectation. A pile of quiet realizations that built into something clear. I didn't want to be pregnant. That much I knew early. The idea of pregnancy, the physical trauma, the risks, the body changes, it all horrified me. And babies? Toddlers? I find them honestly unbearable. They make me nervous, overstimulated, exhausted just by existing near me. I never looked at a baby and felt warmth or longing. Just dread.

I used to say, maybe later. Maybe I'd foster someday or adopt an older kid when I'm done living my 'fun' years. When I've traveled more, healed more, and figured myself out more. That's still on the table, maybe. Because I do like the idea of mentorship, of helping someone already here who needs a home. But that feels like something I'd do from a place of stability and choice, not pressure or expectation. Not because it's 'what comes next.'

My ex and I spent most of our 20s broke, grinding, trying to build a future. But when we finally had money, like when we started going on vacations, living a little, I started to feel this deep knowing of 'I don't want to give this up.' The freedom, the spontaneity, the ability to just be. And when the relationship started unraveling, I thought: If I really wanted kids, I would've had them by now. We were together for over a decade. If I had truly wanted it, I would've made it happen, with him or without him.

But the truth was, I knew I'd be doing all the work. I had lived with him for years. He never once did communal laundry. I cooked, cleaned, and managed everything. We fought constantly about dishes and chores. And I remember saying to him, over and over, why would that magically change if we had a baby? He'd say, "Well, if you were pregnant, I'd do everything. It would be 'Courtney Year.' And I hated that. Why couldn't it just be 'Courtney Year' now? Why did I have to be carrying a baby for him to lift a finger? It made my skin crawl.

And I couldn't stop thinking that if this is how it is with just us, imagine what it would be like with a child. I'd be buried. He'd be applauded for changing a diaper once, and I'd be left to carry the rest. The emotional labor, the domestic work, the loss of self. And that scared me more than anything. Because I watched my own mom disappear after she had kids. She used to say that she lost herself when she became a wife and mother. And I believed her.

The pressure came in waves. Early on, it was constant, 'Where are the grandkids?' Then it eased when I was finishing college and chasing my career. But by my late 20s, it came roaring back. 'You're married, you own a house, you have dogs, why not a baby?' And every time I thought about it, I felt this quiet dread. Like the clock would stop the minute a child arrived. Like my life would end and someone else's would begin, and I'd never get mine back.

Even now, people say, 'Well, you're still young. You have time.' And sure, I do, but do I want to use that time on a decision I already feel this unsure about? Do I want to be 45 dropping a kindergartner off at school? Hell no. And now, newly single at 32, that timeline feels even less appealing. If I meet someone tomorrow, we'd be talking kids in a few years. That puts me at nearly 40. And for what? To squeeze into a mold I never felt called to?

I've seen enough to know that motherhood isn't something you 'try on'. It's a total identity shift. A lifestyle that reshapes every single part of you. And if I'm being honest, I don't think I want that. Not in the way people expect you to. I might want to help someone down the road, to open my home when I'm older and more rooted, but I don't want to lose myself just to check a box.

I used to be scared to admit that. Scared to say the words out loud. Because once you say, I don't want kids, people stop seeing you as 'normal.' They assume you're selfish or just haven't met the right person yet. But that's not it. I've thought about it, like really thought about it. And my answer is no. At least for now. Maybe forever. We shall see."

Chapter 16

Helga's Story - The Space Between Yes and No

Helga and I met a few years ago at work. She was one of the first women I heard voice her questioning of motherhood out loud. It sparked a deep friendship between us with countless conversations on the topic. While I have already arrived at my decision, she is still trying to figure hers out.

"I've been questioning whether I want children for as long as I can remember. Even as a little girl, I assumed the answer would eventually reveal itself. I always assumed it would be like everyone said. That one day, the maternal instinct would just kick in. I'd wake up and suddenly know. That hasn't happened yet. Now, in my early 30s, I'm still waiting for that sense of clarity. Still sitting in the space between yes and no.

Sometimes I see a baby in public or hear a child laughing, and there's a flicker of longing. I imagine holding a tiny hand, watching the first step, shaping a little life with love. I picture what it would be like to be someone's safe place, to witness every milestone. And I know I'd have an incredible partner by my side. My husband would make a wonderful father which is partly what makes this decision so difficult. Sometimes I catch myself imagining what our child would look like, who they'd become, how our partnership would evolve if we became parents.

But then I come home. I settle into the stillness of my peaceful, quiet space, and I remember what I'd be giving up. My independence. My freedom. My calm. The idea of motherhood often feels more romantic in theory than in practice. And when I think about the toll, not just on my time or energy, but on my body and mind, that's when I start to hesitate.

Aside from that, pregnancy and childbirth terrify me. I have a low pain tolerance and a complicated relationship with my own body. A nurse friend once told me, 'Giving birth walks a fine line between life and death.' That sentence has lived rent-free in my brain ever since.

Then there's what comes after. The changes to my body. The risk of postpartum depression. The demands that stretch far beyond the newborn stage. I think about how much I love traveling, how much I need solitude to recharge. Would there be space for those parts of me in motherhood? I'm not sure. And if my child had severe medical or developmental needs, I don't know that I would have the emotional reserves to meet that challenge.

And it's not just the personal sacrifices that give me pause. It's also the world we live in. The political climate makes me feel like my body doesn't even belong to me anymore, like I'm being reduced to an incubator with a deadline. And the environmental crisis weighs on me too. I worry about what kind of planet we're leaving behind. I wonder what kind of future I'd be bringing a child into, and whether that would be fair to them.

I think that's why I feel so caught in the middle. Some days I lean toward yes. Other days I still feel unsure. But then the pressure creeps at reunions or weddings and some extended family asking, 'When are you having kids?' I've never felt pressure from my friends or my mom, and I'm so grateful for that.

But my clock is ticking. I recognize that many women are giving birth to their first later in life now, which is amazing for them. Personally, I would not feel comfortable having my first after the age of 35. Not only do the risks for abnormalities and disabilities start to go up at that point, but I also wouldn't want to put that strain on my body as an older mother. Since I am rapidly approaching my personal cutoff age, the pressure can feel extremely overwhelming at times.

People who don't know me as well might view it as ridiculous, immature, or selfish, but at the end of the day, I only care about the opinions of my closest friends and family. I would rather be absolutely sure before having kids than go into it with reservations and end up regretting my choice. It wouldn't be fair to me or the child.

If I had more time and if the biological clock weren't so loud, I think I'd feel more at peace. But since that isn't an option, I'm learning to give myself grace. I may not know the answer today. But I still have time. And if I ultimately decide not to give birth to a child, there are other ways to nurture, to connect, to love. Adoption could be part of my path someday.

For a long time, it felt like there was no cultural space for women like me, the ones who simply don't know. But I think that's changing. More women are choosing lives outside of motherhood, and that's helping me feel less alone. I see fulfillment in careers, in travel, in friendships, in stillness. There are other ways to build a beautiful life.

And if I never reach a clear decision, well I think that is the decision. It reminds me of that old saying: 'No decision is, in itself, a decision.' But for now, I'm choosing to honor the not knowing."

Chapter 17

Vanessa's Story - When No Found Me

Up next: Vanessa. I don't know Vanessa personally. She was one of the brave strangers who responded to my public call for stories from women navigating this choice. I'm so grateful she chose to share hers. Her journey reminds us that clarity doesn't always arrive loudly or all at once. Sometimes, it creeps in slowly from a place you didn't expect. Vanessa's journey is a powerful reminder that the answer isn't always "no". Sometimes, it's "not now." Or "not this way." Or "not like this." Here's how it found her.

"From a young age, I never really understood the appeal of babies. They always seemed loud and inconvenient to me, and I didn't get why people were so eager to hold them and dote on them.

But people always told me I'd feel differently one day, so I mostly took their word for it. I figured kids would probably happen for me eventually.

In my 20s, I was focused on getting my life off the ground. I told myself I'd only have kids if I had lots of time and money, and secretly, I didn't think those things were likely, so I felt "safe" from ever having to decide.

But then, at 30, my life was kind of perfect. I was making a great living as an author. My schedule was flexible. My husband and I had just bought a big, beautiful house. And suddenly, all those conditions I thought I'd never meet?

I'd met them.

It felt almost stupid not to have kids at that point. And after bonding a bit with my sister's baby, I thought maybe everyone had been right. Maybe it would be different with my own. So, we decided to go for it.

Long story short, I turned out to be infertile.

After years of trying through fertility doctors, medications that made me unbelievably sick, and a mental health spiral I didn't see coming, I had to stop and ask myself:

Is this really worth it to me?

The answer was easy. Absolutely not.

I realized I'd gotten so fixated on solving the infertility 'problem' that I never stopped to ask whether I actually wanted a baby. And the truth was, I didn't. Not really.

So, I told my husband I couldn't keep taking the meds. I told him I didn't think I wanted kids after all.

And lucky for me, he was completely on board. He's a true fence sitter, happy either way and fully supportive of whatever I needed.

I felt a huge weight lift. But it still took me about a year to work through all the societal baggage I didn't even know I'd absorbed.

I worried about being alone when I got old. I worried about how I'd fill all these decades without children.

But over time, I healed. I reframed my life. And I found peace.

I realized you only have to be alone if you choose to be. You can create family and community in your own way. And there is so much to love and look forward to in life without kids.

I got sterilized last year, and I feel more confident and happier with my decision every day. I love my free time. I love my hobbies. I have two spoiled dogs, and my husband and I love to travel.

Life is good."

Chapter 18

Casey's Story - Breaking the Cycle

Casey is another BumbleBFF friend. She and Courtney are key players on our weekly trivia team, "The Bumblebees". She and Courtney came over the other night for drinks and as three childfree women naturally would, we got on the topic of how we all got to our decisions. She grew up in a multigenerational Asian household where family duty and maternal sacrifice were expected. But she decided to break the cycle. Here is what she shared with us that night.

"I've just never had the urge to be a mom. Not once. Not when I was little, not as I got older. Babies, toddlers, teenagers, they've always grossed me out, honestly. Even now, if someone asks, 'What if your brother has a kid and something happens to him? Would you take them in?' My answer is a hard no. I don't even want to adopt. It's just never been in me and it's not going to suddenly appear.

But the truth is, my biggest reason for not wanting kids? My mom. And she doesn't even know that. She thinks it's because I had to babysit growing up or because I liked my independence, but that's not it. Not even close. The real reason is how she treated me. How much it hurt to be her child.

I grew up in a house where I was constantly called ugly and fat. My mom used to say the cruelest things to me. Meanwhile, she'd give all her love and attention to my brother or younger cousin while pushing me away. I have this vivid memory of her literally dragging me out of the house while I held onto the doorframe. I must've been six or seven. She'd kick me out just to spend time with my cousin. It was like she saw no value in me.

I remember asking my grandma on my dad's side once, 'Why does my mom hate me so much?' And she said, 'Because your dad loves you more than he loves her.' That sentence will never leave me.

My relationship with my mom destroyed my sense of safety. Your parents are supposed to be your first safe place, the people who love you unconditionally, who you trust to protect you. But instead, I learned early that love could be manipulative. Conditional. Cruel. I spent years thinking, if this is what having a child looks like, why would I ever risk becoming that?

People talk about generational trauma, and yeah, this was that. My mom's mom treated her the same way. But that doesn't make it okay. Cultural or not, trauma is trauma. And I will not pass it on.

My dad gets it. When I told him I didn't want kids, he said, 'You'd be a good mom, because you know exactly what not to do.' But I still said no. I told him I'm too scared I'd end up like her. Even if I didn't mean to, I couldn't live with myself if I caused a child the kind of pain I lived through.

I wanted to be sterilized as soon as I turned 18. That was the plan. But my parents pushed back. 'You'll change your mind,' they said. Doctors wouldn't take me seriously. So, I stayed on birth control for years. Had I known at the time that it was actually covered by Obamacare, I would have done it.

I honestly forgot about sterilization for a while until I started getting brutal migraines every month. The kind that made me go blind temporarily. My doctor realized they were likely a warning sign of a stroke, which was a risk tied to the birth control. I had to stop immediately. That's when it hit me. I need a permanent solution.

I saw a male doctor first. He pulled all the usual crap: 'Are you sure? What if you want to freeze your eggs?' I said I was sure, but it went nowhere. Then I moved, found a new doctor and I showed up ready to fight for it. I had a whole speech prepared. But she just looked at me and said, 'I believe you. You're old enough to make this decision.' And two days after my 35th birthday, I got it done. It was my present to myself. After that, I just felt like a new person, finally free.

Dating has always been tricky. Guys push back. They think I'll change my mind. Some even cheated because they wanted kids and I didn't. Now I ask right away on the first date, no time wasted. And if they're a fence sitter, I'm out. I know how this goes. They'll get pressure from their parents, start talking about legacy, and eventually, I'll be the one expected to compromise. I'm not doing that dance anymore.

People act like being childfree is cold. But for me, it's one of the most loving things I've ever done. I'm breaking a cycle that harmed me. I'm making sure no child ever has to survive the kind of pain I did. I'm saying no. Not because I don't care, but because I do."

Chapter 19

Margot's Story - The Long View

Margot was the one who truly opened my eyes to what it looks like to live a childfree life. I often think, what if I hadn't moved into that unit in my apartment? I am so happy I did. I met a true friend, a true inspiration. Someone who just by living her life gave me the reassurance I needed. And she never knew it until I wrote this book.

"My name is Margot. I'm 70 years old, and I never had children.

Growing up, I assumed I would. That was just what most women did. You get married, and then you have kids. I never questioned it much in my younger years. I knew I could have children, physically speaking, but I also knew I didn't want to do it alone. And since I never married, the choice kind of made itself.

There was no dramatic crossroads or emotional reckoning. No big announcement. No tears. Life simply moved forward, and I moved with it. I was busy building a career I loved, traveling, forming deep friendships, and filling my life with the things that brought me joy. Somewhere along the way, the window for motherhood quietly closed, and I was completely okay with that.

I worked as a medical nutritionist, and I loved what I did. My career gave me purpose and pride. I've always been academically driven and achievement oriented. I believe in science, health, and helping people. That was my sweet spot. My work wasn't just a job; it became a part of who I was. It kept me curious, challenged, and connected to something bigger than myself.

But that wasn't all my life was. I've always been a social person. I built strong relationships with friends, single, married, with and without children. I've never lacked love, laughter, or a sense of belonging. I made time for joy. I went out, had fun, followed baseball, traveled often, and never once felt like I was missing out on some deeper fulfillment. My life feels full because it is.

I was proposed to twice, but the timing wasn't right. Both men were eager to start families, and I just wasn't there. I didn't want to say yes to something that didn't feel fully right. I'm still friends with both of them, which says a lot. When something isn't aligned, you feel it in your gut. I trusted that feeling. And I've never regretted listening to it.

Coming from a big family (I was one of eight kids) I knew exactly how much work children were. I helped raise my younger siblings. I remember getting up at night to feed my baby brother because my mom, by then in her 40s, was completely exhausted as one would be mothering eight kids. I've been around babies since I was a teenager. That kind of caregiving changes you. It gives you perspective. It shows you what motherhood actually looks like, not just the Hallmark version.

Maybe that's why I've always loved kids without needing one of my own. I've played the role of 'auntie' many times over, helping raise nieces, nephews, and the children of close friends. I've done more than my fair share of babysitting and still do. Watching kids grow into strong, kind adults has been a privilege. And I get to be part of it, just without the full-time responsibility or expense. It's a joy, not a burden. I've always seen it that way.

One of the things I'm most grateful for is that my parents never pressured me to settle down or give them grandchildren. For their generation, that was rare. Despite having eight children of their own, they were more focused on our happiness and success than fitting into tradition. Three of us didn't have kids, and none of us were made to feel 'less than' because of it. That kind of support gave me quiet confidence early on. I didn't have to fight for my choice. I just lived it.

That's not to say people didn't make assumptions. The most common one? That I must be a lesbian because I was unmarried and childless. I never took offense. If anything, I found it amusing. Why is it so hard to believe a woman could simply choose her own path? I didn't feel the need to explain myself then, and I certainly don't now.

In my mid-30s, I chose to get a tubal ligation. My doctor wanted to make sure I wouldn't regret it, but I told her, 'If I ever change my mind, I'll adopt.' There are plenty of children who need loving homes, and I knew I'd be a great mom if life took me in that direction. But it didn't and I've never once looked back or regretted my decision.

Not having children gave me a lot of freedom. I moved where I wanted. I pursued opportunities that may not have been possible if I'd had a family to consider. I prioritized the things that mattered to me. I never felt held back. I never looked at someone else's life and wished it were mine. I was too busy enjoying my own.

These days, I like to joke that I'm on permanent vacation. I'm retired now, but I still travel, spend time with people I love, go to baseball games, and babysit the next generation of littles in my family. I'm active, energetic, and full of life and aging hasn't changed that one bit. My goal is to live long and live well. So far, so good.

My advice? Don't make choices to please someone else. Don't say yes to a lifelong commitment just to fit into someone else's story. Follow your gut. You know yourself better than anyone. And if you don't yet, give yourself the time and space to figure it out. It's your life. Build it with intention.

To any woman wondering whether she'll still be whole without becoming a mother, yes. You will. Your life won't lose meaning. You are still a woman. Your life will still be complete.

And to anyone who questions your decision?

It's none of their damn business."

Section Five: Resolution & Resonance

After hearing from different voices and seeing some different paths, I want to leave you with a few words of encouragement.

The questions have been asked. The doubts explored. The truths, at least in some form, named.

But before we close the book, I wanted to speak directly to a few of you.

To the ones still unsure: you're not doing it wrong. You're just still in it.

To the ones who've decided: your clarity deserves to be honored out loud.

And to the allies, the friends, partners, family members, and quiet champions: thank you for standing beside us, even when the path may look different than your vision.

This final section is a quiet exhale. A few last reflections. A nod to the community that's growing louder every day.

Because no matter where you land, this choice matters.

I THOUGHT ABOUT IT, AND NO.

And so do you.

Chapter 20

You're Not Alone — You're Just Not Loud

Not wanting kids isn't rare. It just tends to be quiet.

You don't see it shouted from rooftops or written on bumper stickers, "Baby Not on Board." There's no "childfree and thriving" aisle at the bookstore. At least not yet.

No national holiday celebrating people who opted out.

No collective narrative that tells you it's okay not to want what everyone else seems to be chasing.

You don't hear, *"I don't want kids"* over brunch with strangers. You hear it in whispers.

You hear it when someone drops their voice and says, *"Me neither."*

Or when someone says, *"I've never told anyone this, but…"*

The decision not to have children isn't a headline. It's not clickbait.

It's not celebrated in Facebook announcements or Instagram reveal photos.

It's personal. Quiet. Sometimes even hidden.

And because of that, you might believe you're one of the only ones.

You're not.

You're not alone. You're just not loud.

Most people don't write heartfelt social media posts about choosing not to have kids.

There are no monthly ultrasound updates when you decide not to reproduce.

No shower gifts. No registries. No "Congratulations on Your Permanent Birth Control" balloons.

But if there were? I'd send one to every woman who's made peace with this decision and to those who are still working on it.

Because the silence around this choice doesn't mean it's shameful.

It just means the infrastructure for celebrating it doesn't exist yet.

The world isn't set up to make this path feel visible.

But that doesn't mean it's not full of people walking it beside you.

The truth is that this decision lives in the background of a lot more lives than you realize.

It lives in:

• The woman who focuses on mentoring, not mothering.

• The couple who travels light and lives large.

• The woman who is taking care of her elderly parents.

• The woman who is a serious boss and climbing her career ladder as high as she wants to go.

• The single friend who loves her quiet mornings and full bookshelf.

• The one who is prioritizing their health.

• The person who considered parenthood carefully...and lovingly chose themselves instead.

You just don't hear their stories as often.

And because you don't hear them, you might think they don't exist.

But they do.

You do.

Some of us were loud about it and learned to be quiet.

We got tired of defending ourselves.

We learned that explaining can become performance, and that not everyone is listening in good faith.

Some of us were quiet and have learned to get louder. Slowly.

Not in an aggressive way. Just in a grounded, confident, I'm-not-ashamed kind of way.

Some of us are still whispering it.

Still wondering if it's okay to say it aloud.

Still practicing what it feels like to sit with that truth without guilt.

That's exactly where I was when I started writing this book.

I wasn't loud about my choice, not even with myself.

I had made a decision, but I still felt isolated inside it.

I went searching for something. A voice, a book, a sentence, anything that would make me feel seen.

And while I found pieces that helped, I never quite heard my own story in them.

So, I wrote the one I needed.

Not because I had all the answers, but because I was still sorting through the questions.

Writing this became its own kind of reckoning. A way to untangle the guilt, the fear, the sadness, the doubt, the freedom, and the relief.

A way to finally say, "This is what I've decided, and it does not make me less than."

If the prologue was my hand reaching out, this chapter is where I turn back to say:

I get it. I was there too.

And maybe, by writing what I couldn't find, I helped create a little more space for all of us to be a little less quiet.

This chapter isn't here to convince you to shout your choice from the rooftops.

You don't owe the world your story.

You don't owe anyone a defense, or a hashtag, or an explanation.

But if you've felt alone in your choice, or your uncertainty, I hope this book reminds you how full the quiet can be.

Because the quiet isn't empty.

The quiet is full of women who have thought about it long and hard and landed on different kinds of joy.

The quiet is full of people who are still deciding. And that too is a valid place to be.

The quiet is full of freedom, grief, peace, ambiguity, and pride. All coexisting.

You may never hear someone say, "Congratulations on not having a child!". But I'll say it here.

Not because you didn't do something, but because you chose.

And choosing what's right for you, even if it's different from what the world expected, is something worth recognizing.

You don't have to be loud to live loudly.

You don't need to shout your decision to feel proud of it.

But if you've ever felt invisible, isolated, or like something must be wrong with you for feeling this way, I hope you carry this with you:

There are more of us than you think.

You're not alone.

You're just not loud.

But we're getting louder.

Chapter 21

A Note to the Ones Still Deciding

If you're still figuring it out, you don't owe anyone your answer yet.

You're allowed to not know.

Maybe the clock is ticking. Maybe your friends are having baby showers. Maybe your doctor brought up egg freezing. Maybe your mom asked you again when she'll get to be a grandma. And maybe you still don't know.

That's okay.

Some people are born with clarity. They've always known they wanted to be a parent, or they've always known they didn't. But most of us live somewhere in between. We toe the line. We circle the question. We say, *"maybe one day"* or *"not yet"* or *"I'm open to it if things feel right."*

There's nothing wrong with that.

This isn't a book that demands a decision from you. This chapter especially isn't. It's a soft place to land, a pause in the noise, and a reminder that confusion doesn't mean failure. You're okay for not knowing.

You're just thinking. And that's a good thing.

There's a lot to think about. More than anyone prepares you for. It's not just about diapers and daycare. It's about identity. It's about what kind of life you want, how you want to spend your time, what kind of energy you have to give, and what kind of world you want to bring someone into.

It's about your:

•Body

•Mind

•Money

•Values

•Support system

•Bandwidth

•Joy

•Loss

•Legacy

•Fear

•Freedom

It's about all the contradictions.

Because this decision is rarely made in isolation. It happens in the middle of a life that's already unfolding. You don't get to press pause on everything else while you figure it out. You still have to go to work. You still have to pay bills. You still have to show up for the people who need you.

You're already carrying so much. You're juggling deadlines, relationships, and maybe a half-dead houseplant.

Some days you might lean toward yes. Other days, no. Some days the thought of raising a child fills you with warmth. Other days it feels like a complete hijacking of your life. You might imagine yourself as a parent and feel possibility. You might imagine yourself childfree and feel relief. Or vice versa. It's not linear. It's layered.

And it's yours.

You don't have to rush toward clarity just to make other people comfortable. You don't have to justify your pause. You don't have to say yes because everyone else did, or no because you're scared of regretting yes.

This is your life. You get to take your time.

And if clarity never arrives like lightning but instead settles in like a quiet knowing, that counts.

If you change your mind, even more than once, that's allowed.

If you freeze your eggs, or don't. If you date someone who does want kids or doesn't. If you stay open, stay curious, stay honest with yourself, that's what matters.

You don't have to prove anything.
You don't have to pick a team.
You don't have to call yourself childfree or future mom or fence-sitter or late bloomer or anything else.

You don't need a label for the sake of closure.

This isn't a club you're in or out of. It's a conversation you are part of.

Somewhere along the way, you might land on your answer. Or it might land on you. One day, you might just wake up and know. Or maybe life will decide for you in ways you didn't expect. Either way, your worth is not attached to your answer.

You are not less evolved, less decisive, or less deserving of support because you're still figuring it out.

This book is here for you too, even if you don't land where I did.

I see you.

And I hope you know that you're not behind.

You're not failing.

You're not alone.

You're just being honest.

And that's brave as hell.

Chapter 22

Living Loud and Childfree

You sifted through the noise, the pressure, the questions, the guilt. You turned down the volume on the world and turned up the volume on your own voice. And now you're here, living a life that's yours. Entirely yours.

Maybe you never wanted kids and owned that early. Maybe it took years of back-and-forth, heartache, or healing. Maybe your path was clear. Maybe it was complicated. But whatever got you here, you made it. And that deserves to be said out loud.

Because childfree isn't a placeholder. It's not a limbo state. It's not something you grow out of or a phase you're supposed to quietly pass through. It's a full, rich, beautiful life. And you're living proof.

You've learned how to fill your days with meaning that isn't rooted in motherhood, even when the world insists that's the only way to matter. You've claimed joy in places people told you you'd never find it. And you've faced the *"you'll regret it"* comments with a clarity that some people spend a lifetime chasing.

Let's be real, it's not always easy. Some days you might still feel invisible. Some days you bite your tongue while others assume you'll change your mind. You might find yourself having to navigate awkward holiday dinners where someone asks when you're having kids, and the whole table turns to you. Or feel left out of certain social circles. But you also have something most people envy: Self-trust.

You trust your gut. You know who you are. And you've given yourself permission to live without an apology.

That's no small thing. In a culture obsessed with babies and family trees, you've carved out your own root system. One rooted in intention, not obligation. One that branches out into friendships, careers, hobbies, animals, travel, art, activism, healing, whatever fills your cup. You've learned to define love beyond biology and legacy beyond lineage.

And I'll say it one more time. You're not broken. You're not bitter. You're not missing out.

You're building. You're contributing. You're thriving.

We need more stories like yours. More women saying, *"I love my life as it is."* More women showing that joy doesn't have to look like minivans and milestone charts. More women saying, *"I choose me."*

So, keep living loud. Keep showing up. For yourself and for the ones still figuring it out. You might not even know they're watching, but they are. Every time you speak your truth, you create a little more room for someone else to speak theirs.

Whether you're single, partnered, dating, divorced, or surrounded by your chosen family, your life is valid. Your love is real.

You get to spend your mornings however you want. You get to rest when your body says rest. You get to pour into the things that light you up, not out of obligation, but out of joy. You get to grow, shift, pivot, dream, build. And no one gets to tell you that your version of life is somehow smaller just because it doesn't include children.

You know better than that.

So, here's to you, the proudly childfree. The ones raising plants, passions, pets, each other. The ones choosing joy over tradition, rest over martyrdom, and truth over performance.

Here's to your freedom. Here's to your peace. Here's to your full, rich, deliberate life.

Remember, you didn't opt out of something. You stepped into something real.

And I hope you never feel the need to shrink it for anyone.

Chapter 23
Advice for Allies

Not everyone reading this book is childfree. Maybe you're a friend, sibling, parent, or partner of someone who is, or maybe you're just curious. Maybe you have children yourself and are trying to understand the women in your life who've chosen a different path. If so, thank you. You're already doing more than most by choosing to listen.

So how can you support the childfree people in your life?

Let's start here — being childfree isn't a phase, a failure, or a problem to solve.

It's a choice.

Or sometimes, a surrender.

For some, it's a joyful declaration.
For others, it's a heavy, hard-earned acceptance.

Either way, it's deeply personal. And yet, society doesn't always treat it that way. In a culture that glorifies parenthood, especially motherhood, being childfree is often treated like an absence. A story unfinished. A glitch in the narrative.

If you want to be an ally, the most important thing you can do is see this path as whole and not lacking. Understand that our lives aren't waiting for a child-shaped puzzle piece to be complete. We aren't missing out on "real love" or dodging "the hardest but most rewarding job in the world." We're simply choosing a different way to build love, meaning, and legacy.

And we're not asking you to agree with every reason or find resonance with every story. We're asking you to respect them. To believe us when we say we're not confused or cruel or lacking. We're complete.

Here are a few ways to be a stronger, more thoughtful ally to the childfree people in your world:

1. Listen Without the Fix-It Face

When someone opens up about not wanting kids, don't tilt your head and say, *"Oh, you'll change your mind."* Don't ask what happened to them. Don't immediately play devil's advocate. That instinct to soothe or reframe can be unintentionally condescending.

What sounds like curiosity often comes off as doubt.

Try this instead:

"Thanks for telling me that."

Or,

"I'd love to hear more if you ever feel like sharing."

135

Treat our decision like you would any other major life choice. With respect, not suspicion.

2. Retire the Bingo Card

You might mean well when you say things like:

- *"You'd be such a good mom."*

- *"You just haven't met the right person yet."*

- *"But don't your parents want grandkids?"*

But these comments, often said with love, land like micro-aggressions. They reduce a complex and deeply personal decision to a misunderstanding, a missed deadline, or a selfish act.

If you wouldn't ask a pregnant woman, *"Are you sure this is a good idea?"*, don't ask a childfree woman, *"But won't you regret it?"*.

3. Stop Framing Parenthood as the Pinnacle

We get it, being a parent is a big deal. But when everything in our culture treats motherhood as the ultimate fulfillment, it leaves little room for other forms of growth and love.

We need allies to recognize that meaning and maturity aren't exclusive to raising children. That nurturing can look like mentoring, art, activism, friendship, or caregiving in other forms. That choosing not to parent doesn't mean opting out of love. It means diversifying it.

Celebrate our milestones like you'd celebrate a baby shower. Join our housewarming parties, book launch parties, garden parties, promotion parties. Cheer for the ways we build our lives. Don't wait for a due date to show up.

4. Don't Make Us the Default Babysitter

If we're close, we might love your kids. We might even offer to help. But please don't assume that our time is more flexible, or our weekends more disposable, because we don't have children of our own.

Just like you, we have commitments, boundaries, and needs. Childfree doesn't mean always available. It means our lives are full in a different way.

5. Watch Your Words Around Kids, Too

You may not even notice when you do it, but children hear you. When you say things like, *"Someday you'll be a mommy,"* or *"When you grow up and have kids…"* you're reinforcing the idea that parenthood is a foregone conclusion. That it's not a choice but rather just a matter of time.

Be the kind of adult who leaves space for kids to become anything. Who asks, *"Do you think you want kids someday?"* instead of, *"How many do you want?"*

Normalize the idea that some people don't want to be parents, and that it's just as valid as those who do.

6. Ask Before You Offer Advice

Even when you're trying to be supportive, avoid jumping in with solutions. Don't suggest freezing eggs, seeing a therapist, or *"just waiting a little longer"* unless invited. Trust that the person you're talking to has considered those options, probably more than you know.

If they want help, they'll ask. Until then, offer your presence, not your prescription.

7. Use Your Voice

Being an ally means speaking up, especially in the rooms we're not in. If you hear someone shaming a woman for not having kids or minimizing her decision, say something. Push back gently but firmly. Use your own experience as a bridge, not a barrier.

And if you're a parent, you have extra power here. Your words carry weight. When you affirm that childfree people are whole and valid, it changes the tone of the room. It tells others that there are many ways to love well and live fully, not just yours.

Bottom Line

We don't need permission to live our lives this way. But support? That's always welcome. Especially when it comes from someone who sees us clearly, not as women who are missing something, but as women who have found what they need.

So, if you're reading this as a friend, a sister, a cousin, a hopeful grandparent, a partner, or just a person trying to understand, thank you for being here.

And thank you for choosing to be the kind of ally who doesn't just say, *"I support you,"* but shows it.

Chapter 24
Let's Keep Talking

This conversation doesn't end here.

In fact, I hope it's just beginning.

Maybe this book gave you language for something you've always felt but never said out loud.

Maybe it helped you feel less strange, less selfish, less alone.

Maybe it made you nod, cry, laugh, rage, or sigh in relief.

Or maybe it cracked open a new question you didn't even realize was sitting in your chest.

Whatever brought you here, I hope you leave knowing this:

Not wanting children is not a flaw to fix.

It's not a phase to grow out of.
It's not a gap in your identity waiting to be filled.
It's a valid, full, and beautiful version of a life.

Being childfree isn't a monologue. It's a chorus.

And it's one we need to keep singing.

So, let's keep sharing our stories.

Let's keep shooting down the Bingos and breaking the silences.
Let's keep making space for nuance, honesty, and joy.
Let's keep talking. Not to defend ourselves, but to honor ourselves.

To anyone who's just beginning this journey: welcome.
To anyone who's halfway through: keep going.
To anyone who's found their answer: live it loudly.

We don't owe anyone an explanation. But we deserve a conversation.

So yes, *I thought about it, and no.*

Acknowledgements

To every woman who shared her story, her voice, or even just her quiet support — thank you. This book exists because of your willingness to speak up, to reflect, and to be honest in a world that too often asks us to stay quiet or explain ourselves.

To the women I interviewed — your stories added depth, humanity, and heart to these pages. I hope you see yourselves in them, and I hope others feel seen because of you. Thank you all for your contribution and bravery.

To my friends, family, and community — thank you for your encouragement, your patience, and your belief in this project (and in me). Your support carried me through the long weekend and late-night writing sessions and the self-doubt that crept in along the way.

And to every reader who picked up this book, whether you're sure, unsure, grieving, proud, or just curious — thank you. I wrote this for you. I hope it gave you comfort, clarity, and maybe even a little courage.

Works Cited

Barroso, Amanda. "How menand women view family life, household duties during COVID-19." Pew ResearchCenter, 25 J a n u a r y 2021,https://www.pewresearch.org/short-reads/2021/01/25/for-american-couples-gender-gaps-in-sharing-household-responsibilities-persist-amid-pandemic/.Accessed 22 July 2025.

Bartlett, Mara. "TheCurrent Price of Parenthood >> globalEDGE: Your source for GlobalBusiness Knowledge." globalEDGE, 5 October 2023,https://globaledge.msu.edu/blog/post/57310/the-current-price-of-parenthood.Accessed 23 July 2025.

Cilley, Constanza. Theright to non-motherhood. 9 November 2 0 2 3 . LatinoAmerica21,https://latinoamerica21.com/en/the-right-to-non-motherhood/.

Cordeiro, Vanessa C."Suicide in children and adolescents." Humanium, 20 November 2023,https://www.humanium.org/en/child-suicide/. Accessed 23 July 2025.

Davis, Maggie. "It Costs$297674 to Raise a Child Over 18 Years." Lending Tree, 13 March 2025,https://www.lendingtree.com/debt-consolidation/raising-a-child-study/. Accessed22 July 2025.

Grimm, Brittany. "Cost ofFreezing Eggs 2023, Egg Freezing Success Rates by Age." New Hope Fertility, 3July 2024, https://www.newhopefertility.com/blog/the-cost-of-freezing-eggs/.Accessed 23 July 2025.

Korhonen, Veera."Percentage of childless women, by age U.S. 2022." Statista, 25 October 2024,https://www.statista.com/statistics/241535/percentage-of-childless-women-in-the-us-by-age/.Accessed 22 July 2025.

Matthews, Alex L., et al."School shootings in the US: Fast facts." CNN, July 2025,https://www.cnn.com/us/school-shootings-fast-facts-dg. Accessed 23 July 2025.

Minkin, Rachel, andJuliana Menasce Horowitz. "Parenting in America Today: A Survey Report (2023)."Pew Research Center, 24 January 2023,https://www.pewresearch.org/social-trends/2023/01/24/parenting-in-america-today/.Accessed 22 July 2025.

Morgan Stanley. "Rise ofthe SHEconomy." Morgan Stanley, 23 September 2019,https://www.morganstanley.com/ideas/womens-impact-on-the-economy. Accessed 1August 2025.

National Institute ofMental Health. "Increases Found in Preteen Suicide Rate - National Institute ofMental Health (NIMH)." National Institute of Mental Health, 30 July 2024,https://www.nimh.nih.gov/news/science-updates/2024/increases-found-in-preteen-suicide-rate.Accessed 23 July 2025.

Oxfam. "Why Oxfam caresabout care." Oxfam, 6 March 2024,https://www.oxfamamerica.org/explore/stories/why-oxfam-cares-about-care.Accessed 22 July 2025.

A Letter to Younger Me

Dear Me,

I know how badly you want answers. You want to get it right. You want to map out your life like a to-do list, with all the boxes neatly checked. You think if you can just plan hard enough, you'll never make a mistake.

But here's the truth: you don't need to have it all figured out right now. In a world where you crave plans, certainty, and control, it's okay to not know. Some decisions are too heavy to make flippantly. This is one of them.

You may wrestle with this longer than you'd like to admit. That does not mean you should regret the choices you've made along the way. Every twist, every delay, every doubt, they will shape you.

And spoiler alert. Your life won't turn out the way you thought it would. But that's okay. Life is a journey. Shit happens. Some decisions you'll make for yourself, and others will be made for you.

It won't always be easy, but you are more than capable of weathering any storm, uncertainty, indecision, grief, or anything else that comes. Don't fight it. Let it be. It's good practice in learning to live with what is, instead of what was "supposed to be".

Never forget who you are and how much love you have to give. And that love is not bound to any one outlet. It goes where you choose.

Above all else, trust your gut. Be bold enough to change your mind. Be brave enough to admit there is no perfect path, no choice that leads to zero regrets. That's not how life works, my dear.

Whatever you choose, whenever you choose it, will be the right decision for you because you are the one who knows yourself best.

With love,

Your future self